A-LEVEL YEAR 2 PSYCHOLOGY FOR EDE

UNIT 2B (Applications: Criminological Psychology)

CRIMINOLOGICAL PSYCHOLOGY STUDY GUIDE

Published independently by Tinderspark Press
© Jonathan Rowe 2018
www.psychologywizard.net

The purchaser of this book is subject to the condition that he/she shall in no way resell it, nor any part of it, nor make copies of it to distribute freely.
All illustrations in this book are Creative Commons.
The author is not affiliated with the Edexcel Exam Board and makes no claim to represent Edexcel's policies, standards or practices.

CONTENTS

CRIMINOLOGICAL PSYCHOLOGY: CONTENT 6

- **BIOLOGICAL EXPLANATIONS OF CRIME** 7
- **INDIVIDUAL, GENDER & DEVELOPMENTAL DIFFERENCES** 21
  - **REVISING EXPLANATIONS OF CRIME** 28
- **UNDERSTANDING THE OFFENDER** 29
- **TREATMENTS FOR OFFENDERS** 33
  - **REVISING UNDERSTANDING/TREATING THE OFFENDER** 38
- **EYEWITNESS TESTIMONY** 39
- **POLICE INTERVIEWS** 44
- **JURY DECISION-MAKING** 50
  - **REVISING EYEWITNESSES, INTERVIEWS & JURIES** 58

CRIMINOLOGICAL PSYCHOLOGY: METHODS 59

- **EXPERIMENTS** 60
- **CASE STUDIES** 63
- **CASE STUDIES USED IN CHILD PSYCHOLOGY** 64
- **SAMPLING** 66
  - **REVISING EXPERIMENTS, CASE STUDIES & SAMPLES** 70
- **METHODOLOGICAL ISSUES IN RESEARCH** 71
- **ETHICS IN CRIMINOLOGICAL PSYCHOLOGY** 77
  - **REVISING METHODOLOGY & ETHICS** 80
- **DATA ANALYSIS** 81
  - **REVISING DATA ANALYSIS & GROUNDED THEORY** 85

CRIMINOLOGICAL PSYCHOLOGY: STUDIES 86

- **CLASSIC STUDY: LOFTUS & PALMER (1974)** 87
- **CONTEMPORARY STUDY 1: BRADBURY & WILLIAMS (2013)** 90
- **CONTEMPORARY STUDY 2: VALENTINE & MESOUT (2009)** 93
- **CONTEMPORARY STUDY 3: HOWELLS *ET AL.* (2005)** 96
  - **REVISING CLASSIC & CONTEMPORARY STUDIES** 99

CRIMINOLOGICAL PSYCHOLOGY: KEY QUESTIONS 100

CRIMINOLOGICAL PSYCHOLOGY: PRACTICAL INVESTIGATION 103

CRIMINOLOGICAL PSYCHOLOGY: ISSUES & DEBATES 106

- **REVISING KEY QUESTIONS, PRACTICALS & ISSUES** 111

ABOUT THIS BOOK

This book offers advice for teachers and students approaching Edexcel A-Level Psychology, Paper 2 (Applications), Topic B (Criminological Psychology). There are two other "applications" to choose from:

- C **Child Psychology**
- D **Health Psychology**

To be clear, candidates only need to answer on ONE of these applications in the exam. There is no expectation that candidates prepare for two or all three of these applications and in fact this is NOT recommended.

Candidates will also need to prepare for the compulsory application:

- A **Clinical Psychology**

Material for Clinical Psychology can be found freely available on the **www.psychologywizard.net** website along with material for Paper 1 (Foundations).

Study Guides for Paper 3 (Issues & Debates) will follow.

> *Text that is indented and shaded like this is a quotation from a researcher or participant. Candidates could use some of these quotations in their exam responses but this is not mandatory.*

Text in this typeface and boxed represents the author's comments, observations and reflections. Such texts are not intended to guide candidates in writing exam answers (i.e. don't go quoting ME!)

TOPIC 2B: CRIMINOLOGICAL PSYCHOLOGY

Criminological Psychology is the study of the mental, social and biological factors associated with criminality and criminal justice. As well as explaining the reasons behind criminal behaviour, it focuses on the reliability of eyewitnesses and jurors and how these can be made more effective.

Criminality is termed OFFENDING BEHAVIOUR because it includes criminal and civil offences and also DEVIANT behaviour which is shocking, upsetting or disruptive but which false short of being illegal (such as nuisance behaviour). In this course, you will be introduced to some of the key questions about offending behaviour: *'What influences people to offend?'* and *'How do psychologists study the behaviour and perceptions of offenders, witnesses and jurors?'* Crucial to answering these questions are SOCIAL NORMS – commonly understood codes of behaviour that may differ from society to society but which influence people to conform. The question is, why do some people ignore these norms?

A key issue in Criminological Psychology is the NATURE/NURTURE DEBATE: are offenders born with an urge to misbehave or is offending behaviour learned from the social environment? This is SOCIALLY SENSITIVE because conclusions about offending influence the way the law is enforced as well as the treatment of minorities.

- **Parents** and **teachers** want to know how best to raise children to be law abiding
- **Police** want to know how to identify offenders, extract confessions from the guilty (but not the innocent!) and help eyewitnesses recall accurately
- **Judges and politicians** want to know how the law can help make sure guilty people are sentenced but innocent people are not – and prevent miscarriages of justice

> *Remember that the title of this unit is "Applications of Psychology" so you should make a point of relating research to these issues: how might families, police and courts respond to these psychological ideas?*

The big debate in Criminological Psychology is the existence of obvious GENDER DIFFERENCES in offending behaviour: in all societies, men commit far more crime than women. There are certainly biological differences between men and women that might explain this, but they are probably overstated: men's and women's brains (for example) are far more similar than they are different.

Many psychologists prefer to explain these differences using Social Psychology, pointing to different NORMS of behaviour and SOCIAL SCRIPTS for males and females (consider the "Bobo Doll" study by Bandura *et al.*). If social factors explain gender differences, perhaps they explain other features of offending behaviour as well.

CRIMINOLOGICAL PSYCHOLOGY: CONTENT

What's this topic about?

This introduces you to the main theories in Child Psychology, in particular the concept of criminal genes, the criminal brain, social theories of CRIMOGENIC (crime-producing) environments or families as well as topics like personality and gender. You will also learn about developmental factors in offending (such as criminal role models, labelling by society and the self-fulfilling prophecy). You will have covered some of these ideas already as part of the AS or Year 1 course:

Social Psychology

Milgram suggests that people have a biological and social reason to obey authority figures, which could include gang leaders and criminal bosses. **Theodor Adorno** proposes the Authoritarian Personality is a type of person who is very conforming but harbours a lot of aggression towards people who are different and this could explain hate crimes. **Sherif's Realistic Conflict Theory** explains why people form hostile groups, which is an explanation of gang crime and hate crime.

Cognitive Psychology

Cognitive Psychology has more to say about the next topic (eyewitness testimony) than explanations of offending behaviour.

Biological Psychology

Raine's study of brain deficits in murderers seems to offer a biological explanation of this type of crime. However, Raine leaves it open whether the murderers were born with these brain deficits or else developed them later in life in response to traumatic life events or social environments. Research into the effects of **testosterone** point towards an explanation of male offending behaviour as a result of aggression and risk-taking. **Evolutionary theory** offers a broader view on this, with aggressive or antisocial traits having some survival value so long as they are not too extreme. **Freud's psychodynamic theory** offers a contrasting explanation of antisocial urges.

Learning Theories

Behaviourists (psychologists like **Watson** and **Skinner**) argue that behaviour is based on STIMULUS AND RESPONSE. John Watson famously claimed that if he was given *"a dozen healthy infants"* he could raise them to be anything he wanted using conditioning techniques, regardless of the child's abilities and this suggests you can raise any child to be a criminal. **Skinner** shows that behaviour is conditioned by rewards (**reinforcements**) and this applies to offending behaviour too, which is often reinforced by stolen goods or simple excitement. **Bandura** in the 1960s went on to show how children develop through observation and imitation and many psychologists are concerned about the amount of violent media that children consume (not just TV and movies, but cartoons and music lyrics too).

BIOLOGICAL EXPLANATIONS OF CRIME

It's been observed for thousands of years that children inherit certain traits from their parents (such as complexion or hair colour) and suspected that they inherit less obvious traits too (such as musical talent or intelligence). In the 19th century, **Charles Darwin**'s **Theory of Evolution** and **Gregor Mendel**'s discovery of **genes** provided a mechanism for this:

- New traits occur because of GENETIC MUTATION during conception
- Some traits have SURVIVAL VALUE if they help a creature survive and reproduce
- These SURVIVAL TRAITS will be passed on to offspring through genes
- Over time, these traits spread through the population, but traits without survival value disappear (this is EVOLUTION THROUGH NATURAL SELECTION)

It's easy to see how giraffes could evolve long necks this way, but how do humans evolve to be criminals? After all, genes evolved long before there were cars or computers or laws against stealing or hacking them. The answer is that there are no 'criminal genes'; genes give us much less-specific instructions:

- **Aggression**, when faced with a threat or with frustration
- **Risk-taking behaviour**, including a lack of fear
- **Lack of empathy** for other people's distress

These traits encourage criminal behaviour, but they also have survival value (because pushy risk-takers who don't care too much about other people's feelings are more likely to have lots of babies who carry on their genes). However, there are limits. Pushy risk-takers are attractive *up to a point* but if they're too extreme, they're less likely to reproduce successfully (because they put potential mates off with their crazy antics, they get themselves killed doing stupid stuff or they get punished by the community).

Long necks are survival traits for giraffes *up to a point*, but, if the neck gets too long, the giraffe suffers injuries and muscle damage. There's an optimal length for a giraffe's neck (6 feet or 1.8 metres) that gets the benefits without the penalties.

Similarly, there's an optimal level of aggression, risk-taking and empathy for dating and mating: one extreme makes you too shy but the other extreme creates social problems.

Most humans are in the middle, with enough aggression and risk-taking to be sexually successful but because of GENETIC MUTATION there are always OUTLIERS (anomalies) with extreme traits and perhaps these are the criminals.

> *You might be thinking about how this ties into stereotypes of women liking 'bad boys' and whether these traits are as important for women attracting partners as men – but we'll return to that when we consider **gender and crime**.*

We're not slaves to our biology: we have FREEWILL (or we think we do). Genes give us a PREDISPOSITION to behave in a certain way (i.e. they 'nudge' us in a particular direction). People can ignore their genetic predispositions, but when you look at large populations these predispositions show up as clear statistical trends.

> *If you have a predisposition towards eating sweet things it doesn't mean you have to eat every chocolate bar you see – but a hundred people with that gene will end up eating more chocolate bars on average than people without that gene.*

Finally, consider that even if you have a predisposition towards aggression, risk-taking and low-empathy, there are all sorts of paths you can take:

- Pushy salesman or saleswoman
- Argumentative politician
- Competitive sports
- Entrepreneur (running own business)
- Soldiers or police officers

Genes don't have a preference for one career over another, so there also seem to be SOCIAL FACTORS at work explaining why people end up as criminals and not politicians.

CESARE LOMBROSO (1876)

19th century Italian doctor **Cesare Lombroso** is known as "the father of modern criminology" for his autopsies on criminals. Lombroso found that criminals had characteristics similar to animals, like apes. In 1876, he published *L'Uomo Dilinquente* ("Criminal Man") in which he argues that criminals are ATAVISTIC: they are lower down the evolutionary scale than "normal" humans: he calls them *"biological freaks"*.

> *The criminal by nature has a feeble cranial capacity, a heavy and developed jaw, projecting [eye] ridges, an abnormal and asymmetrical cranium ... projecting ears, frequently a crooked or flat nose. Criminals are subject to colour blindness, left-handedness is common, their muscular force is feeble* – **Cesare Lombroso**

Lombroso thought these *"born criminals"* were less sensitive to pain and didn't feel remorse (shame/guilt). He also found correlations with excessive tattooing.

Lombroso isn't taken seriously any more but his pictures of atavistic criminals are entertaining

THE 'WARRIOR GENE'

Han Brunner was a geneticist working in a hospital in the Netherlands who studied a Dutch family of criminals in the 1970s, '80s and '90s. The males in the family had a criminal history dating back to 1870, including arson, attempted murder and violent attacks: one had tried to rape his sister, another had tried to run his boss down with a car.

Brunner *et al.* (1993) found that the family suffered from a rare genetic condition that was carried by the females but only affected the males: this defect on the X chromosome reduces the body's production of an enzyme called MONOAMINE OXIDASE-A (MAOA). MAOA normally regulates the production of neurotransmitters like serotonin in the brain. Without this, the men have low IQ and cannot restrain aggressive behaviour.

Brunner Syndrome is rare (only two other families have been discovered with this disorder) but it's less rare for people to have variants where the MAOA-gene is less effective. Since 2004, this has been termed the WARRIOR GENE and is thought to be present in up to 30% of males. However, the MAOA-variant gene has to be 'triggered' (e.g. by a childhood trauma or heavy use of drugs) otherwise it functions normally.

Tilhonen *et al.* (2015) studied 900 criminals in Finland, 78 of them 'extremely violent offenders' who had committed between them 1154 murders, manslaughters and violent assaults. These all carried the low-activity MAOA-variant gene. Those with this gene were found to be 13 times more likely to have a history of repeated violent behaviour

Jari Tilhonen suggests that people with this gene account for up to 10% of all the violent crime in Finland. The 'high risk combination' is for people with the MAOA-variant and CADHERIN-13 (CDH-13) gene (linked to substance abuse and hyperactivity).

> *Studies like this really document that a large percentage of our behaviour in terms of violence or aggression is influenced by our biology - our genes - and our brain anatomy* – **Christopher Ferguson**

XYY SYNDROME

In the '60s, scientists suggested violent crime might be linked to a genetic abnormality, called XYY SYNDROME. Humans have 46 chromosomes, in pairs, one of which determines our sex – XX for females, XY for males. Some unusual males (about 1 in 1000) have an extra Y chromosome. These so-called "supermales" are usually associated with slightly increased height and physical activity and slightly lowered intelligence.

Patricia Jacobs *et al.* (1965) examined 197 Scottish prisoners and found 7 with the XYY chromosomes. This is a higher proportion than exists in the general population. If the extra Y chromosome is responsible for aggressive, antisocial behaviour, then the Y-chromosome in males might explain why criminality is higher in men than women.

Herman Witkin (1976) screened 4591 Danish soldiers but found only 12 cases of the XYY abnormality. These individuals were more likely to have criminal histories than the XY males (41.7 percent compared to 9.3 percent) but not violent or sexual crimes (e.g. shoplifting rather than assault). Witkin concludes that XYY males are only over-represented in prisons because of the way people react to their low IQ and larger physiques – in other words, they are stereotyped and labelled or else exploited by other criminals as 'dupes' or henchmen.

> *Many Psychology websites and books wrongly muddle XYY Syndrome with Klinefelter Syndrome. Klinefelter is having an extra X chromosome, a completely different condition. My thanks to Rav Grewal for correcting me on this.*

STUDIES INTO BRAIN DAMAGE

Interest into criminality and the brain begins with **Phineas Gage**. In 1848, an accident with dynamite blasted a "tamping iron" (a metre-long iron nail) through Gage's skull; it entered through Gage's cheek, passed through his brain and shot out of the top of his head.

Amazingly, Gage survived the accident, thanks to treatment from **Dr John Martyn Harlow**. However, his personality changed: he became obscene, rude and reckless whereas before he had been very responsible.

Phineas Gage poses (with the tamping iron that injured him) in 1860

In his **case study**, Harlow reported that Gage became

> *fitful, irreverent, indulging at times in the grossest profanity (which was not previously his custom), manifesting but little deference for his fellows, impatient of restraint or advice when it conflicts with his desires* – **John Harlow (1868)**

After he died, 12 years later, Gage's skull was preserved and studied. Modern computer-assisted design has reconstructed the damage to his brain: it was damage to the frontal lobe, which is responsible for decision-making and self-restraint.

> *Amazingly, Phineas Gage's skull was preserved as a curiosity after he died. The skull and the tamping iron are on display at Harvard Medical School in the USA.*

Phineas Gage's injury links to research by **Adrian Raine** into brain differences in murders. 41 killers pleading Not Guilty By Reason of Insanity (NGRI) were matched with non-criminal Controls and given a PET scan. The NGRIs showed less activity in the **frontal lobe** (where Gage was damaged) and **corpus callosum** but increased activity in the **right anterior amygdala**.

> *You learned about **Raine et al. (1997)** as the classic study in the **Biological Approach** for Unit 1. It would be a good idea to revise this now.*

Other studies support this link. **Yang et al.** (2009, Adrian Raine was a researcher in this study too) used **MRI** scans to compare 27 PSYCHOPATHS (*c.f.* p22) with 32 non-criminal controls. They found that the psychopaths had smaller amygdalas (17.1% smaller in the left hemisphere and 18.9% small in the right hemisphere, on average).

Moreover, there was a significant correlation between the size of the reduction and the psychopaths' score on the HARE PSYCHOPATHY CHECKLIST (PCL). **Yaling Yang** suggests that the amygdala helps restrain antisocial behaviour, so when it is smaller people have less self-control.

- Psychopaths have an unusual **personality** that makes it hard for them to have **empathy** for other people. They are considered in more detail on pp22-23.

Glenn et al. (2009 – and Adrian Raine was a researcher on this too!) gave 17 **psychopaths** moral problems to solve (e.g. *"Should you keep money you found in a lost wallet?"*) while scanning them using **fMRI**. Not only is the amygdala smaller in psychopaths, it's also less active during moral decision-making. **Andrea Glenn** concludes that psychopaths don't worry as much as other people about harming others when making moral decisions.

EVALUATING BIOLOGICAL EXPLANATIONS OF CRIME AO3

Credibility

Early research by **Lombroso** seemed to have credibility at the time because of the link to **Darwin's Theory of Evolution**, which backs up the idea that behaviour is inherited. However, as scientists came to understand evolutionary theory better, the idea of body types being linked to morality and crime lost credibility (p75).

Instead, improved understanding of **genes** focused on how they interact to favour PREDISPOSITIONS like risk-taking or aggression. These predispositions can (but don't have to) direct people towards crime. Studies like **Tilhonen et al. (2015)** are far more credible because they show people being 'at risk' of becoming criminals due to their genes, but not driven to crime against their freewill.

Finally, the development of brain imaging techniques improves the credibility of theories about brain damage and brain dysfunction. **fMRI** is particularly valuable because it shows brain activity as well as the size of brain structures.

Objections

Lombroso's idea that criminals are 'less evolved' than other people and more like animals is a misunderstanding of Darwin's Theory. Lombroso failed to take into account how the poor appearance of criminals could be the *result* of a life of poverty, poor diet and disease rather than the cause of a criminal lifestyle.

The biggest problem for all this research is the definition of criminality itself. Since laws differ from country to country and change over time, a person who is a criminal in one country or one decade might not be a criminal somewhere else or at another time. For example, rape within marriage only became a crime in the England & Wales in 1991 (1989 in Scotland); whereas homosexuality was a crime in England & Wales until 1967 (1981 in Scotland). Therefore, the location and date of a study will affect who is and who isn't a criminal.

Some studies (e.g. **Tilhonen et al.**) focus on severe crimes of violence, others (e.g. **Mednick et al.**) include any sort of criminal record at all (such as drink-driving) and some (e.g. **Bohman**) specifically focus on petty crime such as shoplifting. **Witkin** found that XYY Syndrome only linked to petty crime and perhaps for reasons more to do with society than biology.

Research only focuses on criminals who have been convicted of crimes. In the UK, 70% of crimes are undetected (source: *The Independent*, 2013) which makes creating a non-criminal Control group very unreliable. **Michael Naughton (2002)** points out that, during the 1990s, 770 criminal convictions were successful appealed every year in the UK so studies probably contain some innocent people in their criminal groups as well.

Differences

In the 20th century, LABELING THEORY (**Becker, 1963**) suggests that we tend to act based on how other people treat us, so if we're unfortunate enough to look untrustworthy, aggressive or evil, other people will be prejudiced against us and we may end up behaving badly due to the SELF-FULFILLING PROPHECY (SFP).

The **case study** of Phineas Gage could also be due to SFP, since everyone treated Gage differently after his accident had disfigured him. Other critics question whether Gage's personality really did change. Other than **Harlow**'s anecdotes (written 20 years after the incident), there's no evidence that Gage became a criminal, a drunk or a drop-out.

Furthermore, the failure of twin studies to find 100% concordance in MZ twins over criminality suggests something other than biology is also at work. Even the theory of the WARRIOR GENE admits that traumatic triggers are needed to activate the MAOA-variant gene – such as drug abuse or violence, meaning that lifestyle is as important as biology. Moreover, many people commit crimes who **don't** have the warrior gene, so that cannot be a complete explanation.

The advantage that non-biological explanations have is that they explain crimes other than those based on aggression or risk-taking or lack of empathy. For example, there are 'victimless' crimes that don't involve aggression (like tax evasion) and crimes with very little risk to the criminal (e.g. in 90% of bicycle thefts and burglaries, no suspect is even identified, according to the Home Office in 2017).

Applications

Despite the advances in genetic science, we are still a long way from being able to SCREEN the population to determine who does or who doesn't have certain genes or brain structures. Even if we could, simply possessing these biological characteristics doesn't guarantee you will become a criminal. **Adrian Raine** points out that he himself has a 'murderer's brain' but went on to become a psychologist not a criminal.

A more practical use for these discoveries is in risk assessment. For example, parole boards have to decide whether it's safe to release a prisoner and currently this is done through interviews (by psychiatrists and social workers) and observations (by prison staff). Information like brain scans or genetic tests could help parole boards so that they are less likely to release someone who will be a danger to the public.

Similarly, when a criminal is convicted a judge has to decide whether to issue a CUSTODIAL SENTENCE (e.g. prison). Information from brain scans and genes could inform this decision, so that judges imprison dangerous offenders but give non-custodial sentences (like community service) to offenders who don't pose a risk.

SOCIAL EXPLANATIONS OF CRIME

Most criminal behaviour is **social behaviour**: it's done by a group of people and targets other groups of people. Other than very rare serial killers, most criminals are *not* lone individuals and they encourage each other in various ways:

- **Authority Figures:** There are criminal authority figures (e.g. gang leaders, crime bosses, terrorist leaders) who order their followers to carry out criminal acts
- **Criminal In-Groups:** There are criminal gangs who see themselves as an **in-group** and view law-abiding people as **out-groups**. There are also HATE CRIMES specifically targeting people the criminals view as out-groups because of their race, religion, gender or sexuality.

*These social theories were introduced in **Unit 1** so this would be a good point to go back and revise **Migram, Latané, Sherif** and **Tajfel**.*

LABELLING THEORY

Social labels are stereotypes that get attached to individuals or whole groups of people. They can be positive (e.g. 'hard-working' or 'clever') but they can also be negative ('lazy' or 'stupid'). Criminal labels include 'thief', 'thug' and 'rapist'. A negative label is known as a STIGMA; being given a negative label is being STIGMATISED (**Goffman, 1963**).

In his study of medical misdiagnosis, **David Rosenhan** refers to "*the stickiness of labels*" – once a label has been attached, it affects the way everyone else sees that person and interprets their behaviour; it's hard to do things that 'disprove' the label so labels are very hard to remove.

Rosenhan (1973) is the classic study for Clinical Psychology (Unit 2A) so it would be a good idea to revise this now.

Howard Becker (1963) points out that certain labels have MASTER STATUS: they are noticed by everybody, they affect the way almost everyone views you and they are very difficult to challenge. Gender, race and religion are all examples of labels with master status, but criminality is another.

- Money goes missing all the time, but if someone in the group has been labelled a 'thief' then the missing money will be regarded as stolen
- People are always having disagreements, but if someone has the label 'thug' their argumentativeness will be viewed as threatening
- Lots of people show an interest in the opposite sex (or the same sex!) but if someone has the label 'rapist' the interest they show will produce alarm and anger

Labels can be RETROSPECTIVE (where the past is reinterpreted) or PROJECTIVE (where expectations about the future are altered):

- Once some gets the label 'thief', their friends and neighbours will look back on other occasions when money went missing and reinterpret these things, not as accidents, but as theft (RETROSPECTIVE).

> *This links with the **Schema Theory** of **Bartlett (1932)** which you studied as part of Cognitive Psychology in Unit 1. You should revise the idea of schemas now.*

- Around someone with the label 'thief', people keep a close eye on their possessions and if stuff goes missing they will regard it as theft rather than carelessness (PROJECTIVE)

> *Labelling people as out-groups is a form of projective labelling: you expect out-group people to be odd, unfriendly, untrustworthy. This is shown in the study by **Tajfel (1970)** who found Bristol schoolboys would be less generous towards outgroup members.*

Labels can be applied in a very arbitrary way. **Edwin Lemert (1972)** points out that everyone commits deviant and antisocial acts all the time: taking a towel from a hotel, a pen from the office, downloading a pirated song or movie, breaking the speed limit, under-age drinking or smoking, etc. However, only a minority of people get caught and punished for doing these things: these people get the stigma of 'criminal'. Lemert calls this SECONDARY DEVIANCE: the deviant behaviour that society actually notices and reacts to.

- You can get the label of 'thief' quite accidentally: taking something you thought was 'just lying around', taking something you intended to return, being in the wrong place when something valuable went missing.

> *The 1986 film 'Stand By Me' (dir. Rob Reiner) has a powerful scene in which 12-year-old Chris Chambers (River Phoenix) weeps with frustration because his label of 'thief' means no one will believe him when his teacher steals the milk money and blames it on him: he sobs, "I just wish I could go some place where nobody knows me!" Watch it on YouTube.*

- Since whole groups can be stigmatised (e.g. races, social classes), individuals from stigmatised groups who don't behave any differently from anyone else are still more likely to be caught and labelled with secondary deviance

Aaron Cicourel (1968) points out that some people can NEGOTIATE their label. To do this you need to have influence and be articulate. In general, wealthy and educated people are better able to negotiate their labels and are less likely to be stigmatised than poor and uneducated people.

For example, at the time of the London Riots in 2011, the London mayor (Boris Johnson) and UK Prime Minister (David Cameron) had been part of a 'gang' at Oxford University called the Bullingdon Club. The Club had a reputation for 'trashing' bars and restaurants as well as university property. However, wealthy Club members were not expelled or arrested and were treated as young people 'letting off steam' in contrast to the London rioters who were given tough criminal sentences.

This theory is linked to a concept in Sociology called SOCIAL CONSTRUCTIONISM. This is the idea that crime and deviancy are created by attitudes in society. In effect, society 'creates' criminals by the way it labels people.

Sytske Besemer *et al.* (2013) investigated OFFICIAL BIAS (the way that police and the courts pay more attention to people from certain stigmatised backgrounds and 'problem families'). They used data from the **Cambridge Study in Delinquent Development (CSDD)** which is a famous **longitudinal study** following 411 working class boys from London from their birth in 1953 throughout their lives. They found that the strongest predictor for one of the participants getting a criminal record was having a parent with a criminal record and coming from a low income/poor housing family. This supports the idea that labelling is responsible for people becoming criminals.

SELF-FULFILLING PROPHECY (SFP)

Labelling Theory explains why people get *treated* as criminals, but it doesn't explain why they *act* unusually. For instance, it's just not true that we are all equally criminal in our behaviour but the police and courts only pick on some of us but not others; there are burglars, murderers and rapists who do things that other people in society don't do.

One explanation is the what **Robert K. Merton (1948)** terms the SFP or **'Pygmalion Effect'** which explains how we start to see ourselves based on the by other people teat us; eventually we actually turn into the very thing we've been labelled as: this is why prophecies (predictions, labels) can be 'self-fulfilling'.

> *Pygmalion is the name of a play by George Bernard Shaw that was made into a musical called 'My Fair Lady'. In the story, a poor London flower-seller named Eliza Doolittle is the subject of a cruel experiment to see if she can be trained to pass for an aristocratic lady. However, Eliza's personality changes when people start treating her differently.*

According to SFP, we get our SELF-IMAGE from the way other people in society respond to us. Our self-image then influences our ACTIONS and our actions then cause other people's SOCIAL REACTIONS to change. This is based on what **Charles Cooley (1902)** calls the LOOKING-GLASS SELF: we get our idea of our 'self' or personality by INTERNALISING the way society treats us.

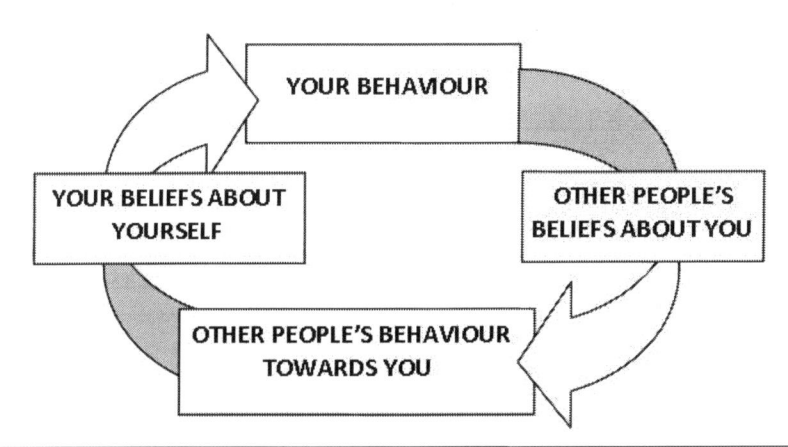

```
        YOUR BEHAVIOUR
YOUR BELIEFS ABOUT          OTHER PEOPLE'S
    YOURSELF                BELIEFS ABOUT YOU
        OTHER PEOPLE'S BEHAVIOUR
              TOWARDS YOU
```

Make a point in the exam of illustrating this diagram with examples: if you take drugs, other people think of your as untrustworthy, they stop including your in their pastimes, you start to see yourself as an outsider so you move on to dealing drugs or other types of crime.

A famous study in SFP is **Rosenthal & Jacobson (1968)** who carried out a field experiment on children at Oak School in California. They gave the pupils an IQ test and told the teachers that the tests identified some of the children as 'bloomers' who would do well at school. In fact, the 'bloomers' had been picked at random but the teachers didn't know this.

At the end of the school year, the researchers tested the children again and found that the 'bloomers' really had shot ahead of the rest of the class, making the biggest improvement in scores.

The change in scores was due to the teachers treating the 'bloomers' differently from the other pupils: paying more attention to them, praising their work, having high expectations. This is a good example of the SFP in action.

Stephanie Madon applied the SFP to negative behaviour (underage drinking) rather than positive behaviour. **Madon et al. (2004)** tested 115 American 12-year-olds: first their parents were asked to predict how much alcohol the children would drink over the coming year, then a year later the children were interviewed about their own drinking.

- The children who drank the most alcohol were the ones whose parents made the highest predictions
- A single parent having a negative view of the child (high prediction) correlated with more drinking
- Both parents holding negative views correlated with the most drinking

This suggests the children INTERNALISE their parents' negative views of them: classic SFP. In an earlier (**2003**) study, Madon found that positive labelling by mothers had a bigger effect on children than negative labelling, especially on children with high SELF-ESTEEM (i.e. a positive self-image, not looking down on themselves).

An unusual study of SFP was carried out by **Gustav Jahoda (1954)** who researched the Ashanti people of Ghana, Africa. The Ashanti have a tradition giving boys a 'soul name' based on the day of the week they are born. Boys born on Wednesdays are named '*Kwaku*' and the belief is that they grow up to be bad-tempered and violent, whereas boys born on Mondays (named '*Kwadwo*') will be peaceful and gentle. By studying court records of 1000 delinquents, Jahoda found that boys named '*Kwaku*' accounted for 22% of the reported crimes, compared to 6% for boys named '*Kwadwo*'.

This seems to show SFP happening across a whole society, with negative labelling of boys with a certain name leading to increased delinquency in later life.

> *Jahoda became a friend of **Henri Tajfel** who developed **Social Identity Theory** which explores the way we treat people differently based on the social group we view them as belonging to*

The opposite of the SFP is the SELF-DEFEATING (or SELF-DENYING) PROPHECY, also known as 'reverse psychology'. This is when the prophecy PREVENTS the prediction from coming true. For example, a teacher predicts a student will fail a test but this makes the student determined to prove their teacher wrong, so they study even harder and pass. Some people from stigmatised backgrounds know that people expect them to become criminals, but this makes them determined to do the opposite.

- Why are some people influenced by the SFP to **become** criminals due to stereotypes, discrimination and stigma?
- Why are other people motivated by the SDP to **avoid** criminality despite those stereotypes and stigma?

Individual Differences (e.g. personality) might be an important factor in this. People who score high for NEUROTICISM are more likely to INTERNALISE negative labels (SFP) whereas STABLE personalities will rest negative labels (SDP).

EVALUATING SOCIAL EXPLANATIONS OF CRIME AO3

Credibility

These theories are supported by both **correlational research** (such as the **CSDD, Jahoda, Besemer et al.** and **Madon et al.**) which points to patterns or trends in society and also **experimental research** (such as **Rosenthal & Jacobson**) which shows cause-and-effect, with social situations causing prosocial or antisocial behaviour.

The **Cambridge Study in Delinquent Development (CSDD)** has generated a huge amount of longitudinal data about CRIMOGENIC (crime-causing) factors in upbringing and environment. Since 1969, it has been directed by **David Farrington**.

The CSDD draws particular attention to family background, poverty and upbringing as factors linked to crime.

Taken together, this research suggests we are social animals and that what makes offenders different from law-abiding people is not their biology but their social environment.

Weaknesses

Many of these studies are on children, which tell us a lot about development but can't necessarily be generalised to adults, who might be much less influenced by labels.

Most of these studies aren't investigations into *crime*, just antisocial behaviour, rule-breaking or going against your conscience. Now crime usually involves being antisocial, breaking rules and going against the conscience, but lots of things that aren't crimes involve these things too (like cheating on your partner or gossiping about a friend). These studies explain why people are "bad" but not why they choose a life of crime.

Research into labelling doesn't prove that people act on their labels. The parents in **Madon et al.** might just be very good judges of their children's secret drinking habits and **Jahoda**'s study only shows that courts discriminate against boys named *Kwaku*, not that these boys actually behave worse than other children.

Not all crimes come from a social stigma. Serial killers are usually law-abiding in other ways; 'WHITE COLLAR CRIME' is carried out by wealthy and privileged people (such as cheating on taxes and embezzling their company's money) who also have positive labels.

The CSDD only looks at working class boys and working class backgrounds are the overwhelming focus in Criminological Psychology which could be seen as discrimination.

Differences

Social explanations can be contrasted with biological explanations that are DISPOSITIONAL (they identify the cause of offending *within* the offender rather than in the environment). There could be biological explanations for this (e.g. the prefrontal cortex or the amygdala).

Biology might explain why not everyone acts according to SFP (and some respond to SDP instead) and why some people can negotiate negative labels but other people just internalise them.

Furthermore, many people commit crimes who ***don't*** have the WARRIOR GENE (p9), so biology cannot be a complete explanation either.

The CSDD's surprise finding was the importance of **personality** in offending, especially IMPULSIVENESS (acting without thinking) which links to being EXTRAVERTED (p21).

The advantage that social explanations have is that they explain 'victimless' crimes that don't involve aggression (e.g. tax evasion) and crimes that are NON-UTILITARIAN (crimes that don't gain you money or physical reward): offenders are acting out their labels and internalising a self-image that they are "bad".

Applications

Labelling theory suggests that it is better to deal with young delinquents by *not* giving them criminal records which turn into SELF-FULFILLING PROPHECIES (SFP, p16). The UK Government tried a strategy called **Antisocial Behaviour Orders (ASBOs)** between 1998-2014. These involved dealing with delinquents by giving them a sort of 'contract' with a social worker and only criminal convictions as a last resort.

Unfortunately, ASBOs became a powerful label in their own right (some delinquents viewed them as a 'badge of pride') and the scheme was viewed as a failure.

Other criminologists favour the "short, sharp shock" approach of putting delinquents in military-style 'boot camps'. It is hoped the unpleasant experience will trigger the **Self-Defeating Prophecy (SDP, p18)**, making the young offenders determined to change their ways.

Treatment for young offenders often focuses on using COGNITIVE BEHAVIOURAL THERAPY (CBT) to build SELF-ESTEEM and a positive self-image. This helps young people resist negative labels (as found by **Madon *et al.*, 2003**) and makes the SDP more likely rather than SFP.

FURTHER REFLECTIONS

The likelihood is that both biology *and* social pressure combine to cause criminal behaviour. This is an INTERACTIONIST approach (because biology and environment interact differently for each person). This would explain why twin and adoption studies don't find 100% concordance and why sometimes the SFP and sometimes the SDP occurs when people are labelled.

One factor that MEDIATES (comes between and settles) biological and social factors is the concept of PERSONALITY or DISPOSITION. This is a person's temperament that enables them to resist some pressures but perhaps makes them more vulnerable to others. **Hans Eysenck (1964**, p21) argues that NEUROTIC-EXTRAVERTS are more likely to be criminals because they crave excitement but don't learn from their past mistakes.

Another mediating factor between biology and environment is SELF-ESTEEM or positive self-image. **Mier & Ladny (2017)** carried out a meta-analysis of 42 studies over 25 years and found a **negative correlation** between self-esteem and youth offending (with low self-esteem correlating with increased offending). This might be because self-esteem helps young people resist labels or resist biological urges or (probably) both.

INDIVIDUAL, GENDER & DEVELOPMENTAL DIFFERENCES

Social and biological explanations of crime assume that we are all affected equally by environment, genes or brain structure, but this doesn't seem to be the case. Research into labelling or deindividuation shows that some people resist social pressures – while others offend without any apparent social pressure at all. Similarly, not everyone with a genetic or neurological (brain-based) PREDISPOSITION becomes an offender.

These qualities that cause people to 'buck the trend' are INDIVIDUAL DIFFERENCES.

PERSONALITY DIFFERENCES

One of the most famous researchers into personality is **Hans Eysenck**, a psychologist who fled the Nazis and came to Britain in the 1930s and studied the effect of war on soldiers. Eysenck proposed two basic DIMENSIONS of personality

- **EXTRAVERSION (E):** a need for stimulation found by being in company, being the centre of attention and taking risks (people who score low on E are **'introverts'** so this is sometimes called the **extraversion-introversion scale**)
- **NEUROTICISM: (N):** a tendency towards quickly-changing moods and seeing situations as threatening (people who score low on N are **'stable'** so this is the **neuroticism-stability scale**)

Everybody can be described by these two traits, having varying degrees of E and N:

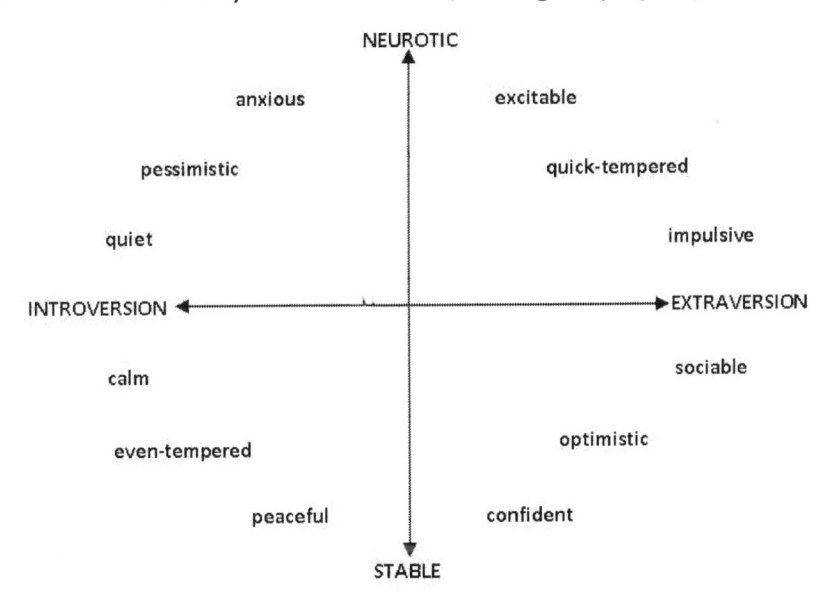

```
                        NEUROTIC
                           ▲
         anxious                    excitable
      pessimistic                 quick-tempered
         quiet                       impulsive
INTROVERSION ◄─────────────┼─────────────► EXTRAVERSION
          calm                        sociable
      even-tempered                  optimistic
          peaceful                    confident
                           ▼
                         STABLE
```

Eysenck proposes that E and N are 25% environment and 75% biology:

- **EXTRAVERSION** is based on the body's RETICULAR ACTIVATING SYSTEM (RAS) which acts as a 'thermostat' regulating how much stimulation the brain gets. The RAS is weak for strongly-extraverted people, so they seek stimulation from their environment; strongly-introverted people have a powerful RAS and are easily 'overloaded' with stimulation, which is why they prefer quiet
- **NEUROTICISM** is based on the body's AUTONOMIC NERVOUS SYSTEM (ANS) which governs the 'FIGHT-OR-FLIGHT' response to threat. A highly sensitive ANS reacts to changes as threats, producing unstable emotions.

Eysenck (1964) proposed that the criminal personality is neurotic-extravert (high-N and high-E) because these people are impulsive thrill-seekers who do not learn from past experience (i.e. punishment and bad consequences don't make them change their ways, nor are they strongly affected by reinforcement).

Eysenck later (**1966**) added a third trait: PSYCHOTICISM

- **PSYCHOTICISM:** lacking in empathy, insensitive to other people, uncaring about social approval (scoring high on P makes you callous and cruel but also creative and artistic; low-P scores indicate compassion and a need to fit in to society)
- **PSYCHOTICISM** is based on the body's HORMONES, especially testosterone (the male growth hormone linked to aggression).

> *Beware. In everyday language, 'psychotic' often refers to someone out-of-control and wild. Eysenck's **psychoticism** is different from this: he is referring to cold, antisocial persons who have no sense of shame – not raving lunatics!*

Together, these 3 traits make the PEN MODEL OF PERSONALITY. The EYSENCK PERSONALITY QUESTIONNAIRE (EPQ) is a **psychometric test** with 100 yes/no questions that scores P, E and N. **Eysenck (1966)** studied 2070 male prisoners and compared their EPQ scores to 2422 male controls. Eysenck's prisoners scored higher on P, E and N.

However, **Farrington et al. (1982)** reviewed 16 studies and found that overall the prisoners scored higher on P, but not on E and N.

PSYCHOPATHY

More recent psychologists have moved away from Eysenck's ideas to focus on PSYCHOPATHS. Psychopaths are individuals with a collection of traits, especially EGOTISM (selfishness and a lack of concern for how other people view them), a LACK OF EMPATHY for other people's feelings and MANIPULATIVE BEHAVIOUR.

> *Beware again! Everyday language often uses 'psychopath' to describe someone outrageously destructive and cruel, like Hannibal Lecter or the Joker, but psychopaths don't have to be outrageous or violent – although those that **are** can be responsible for the worst crimes.*

A key researcher into **psychopathy** (pronounced *sy-KOP-pathy*, not *syko-PATH-y*) **is Dr Robert Hare**, who created a psychometric test to score psychopathy. The PSYCHOPATHY CHECKLIST (PCL) scores respondents 0, 1 or 2 on 20 descriptions. Anyone scoring 30+ out of 40 might be a psychopath.

- **Glibness:** superficial charm without sincere feelings
- **Grandiosity:** a huge sense of self-importance and superiority
- **Irresponsibility:** blaming others for your own problems
- **Lack of remorse:** no shame or guilt for bad behaviour
- **Parasitic lifestyle:** taking advantage of other people, e.g. multiple marriages, sexual cheating, broken parole

A high-scoring psychopath views the world in a very different way. It's like colour-blind people trying to understand the colour red, but in this case 'red' is other people's emotions – **Robert Hare**

Psychopathy doesn't automatically make you a criminal. In fact, it could make you very successful in other ways. **Babiak & Hare (2006)** tested 203 executives in big American corporations and found 4% scored 30+ on the PCL: they were *"workplace psychopaths."* In the general population, psychopaths are estimated to be 1%. However, **Babiak et al. (2012)** found 15-20% of the 2 million prisoners in the USA to be psychopaths.

Try the test yourself at **http://vistriai.com/psychopathtest/**

Blair et al. (1996) tested 11 psychopathic prisoners (as determined by the PCL) at the Broadmoor Psychiatric Hospital in the UK. They compared them to 14 non-psychopathic prisoners. All were serving life sentences for murder or manslaughter and were matched for IQ and ethnicity. The prisoners watched a slideshow of 28 slides: mixed in were 5 **distressing images** (e.g. a baby crying, a wound) and 5 **threatening images** (e.g. a shark, a gun). Polygraph machines were used to measure GALVANIC SKIN RESPONSE (slight changes in perspiration on fingertips) which indicates physical arousal due to alarm.

The psychopaths showed the same skin response as the non-psychopaths to the threatening images but not to the distressing images. However, the psychopaths *claimed* to find the distressing images troubling, but their skin response showed this to be untrue. This illustrates both **lack of empathy** and **manipulation/glibness**.

GENDER DIFFERENCES

One of the most striking features of criminal behaviour is that it is overwhelmingly done by men. Male criminals outnumber women 4-to-1 and also commit more serious crimes. In the USA, 93% of prisoners are male; in the UK, it is 95% and the global average is 96% (source: **International Centre for Prison Studies, 2015**).

There are many possible explanations for these gender differences:

- **Risk-taking & aggression:** Antisocial traits might have SURVIVAL VALUE in males (to attract mates and fight off rivals) but not so much in females
- **Brunner Syndrome:** Genetic disorders like **Brunner Syndrome** (p9) are carried by females but only show symptoms in males
- **XYY Syndrome:** If XYY Syndrome (p10) really does link to criminality, then males might be more prone to crime simply because they have a Y chromosome.
- **Brain Injury:** There is evidence that males are more at risk than females for TRAUMATIC BRAIN INJURY (TBI; source: **NHS, 2015**) and research by **Adrian Raine** and case studies like **Phineas Gage** (p10) link TBI to criminal behaviour
- **Personality Differences:** Women score higher on **Neuroticism** but men score higher on **Psychoticism** (**Eysenck, 1975**, p21); this finding is supported in a study of 37 countries by **Lynn & Martin (1997)**
- **Different Labels:** women are more affected by FORMAL LABELLING (by teachers, bosses, etc) and by negative labels from family (based on a study in female offenders in Trinidad by **Ramoutar & Farrington, 2006**)
- **Social scripts**: Society tolerates (even encourages) deviant behaviour in men, but young girls are expected to follow a SOCIAL SCRIPT of caring for others and conforming to rules. **Bandura *et al.* (1961, p25)** noticed that boys were more likely to imitate physical aggression than girls and he links this to social scripts.
- **Chivalry Hypothesis:** This is the idea that the CRIMINAL JUSTICE SYSTEM (CJS) treats women more leniently than men, so female criminals exist but are less likely to be arrested or convicted.

However, gender differences in criminal behaviour might be disappearing because of changes in society. **Rita Simon (1975)** proposes EMANCIPATION THEORY: increasing equality for women makes them as crime-prone as men and the CJS treats men and women offenders more equally. In support of this, the numbers of women offenders has been rising in the UK since the 1950s. However, the CONVERGENCE (growing similarity) of male and female crime rates might be less to do with women becoming more like men and more to do with men becoming more 'feminine' and less violent and antisocial.

DEVELOPMENTAL DIFFERENCES

Parents have high hopes for their babies and don't want them to grow up to be criminals; society puts out strong messages to children that crime is bad, rules should be followed and goodness will be rewarded. However, some children develop into offenders. What goes wrong?

- **Biological Explanations:** Children born with the WARRIOR GENE or receiving TRAUMATIC BRAIN INJURY (TBI) at an early age may struggle with **impulsivity** (acting without thinking) and a **lack of empathy**. This means they won't be successfully CONDITIONED into law-abiding behaviour.

- **Social Labelling:** Children can be given a STIGMA at an early age and then INTERNALISE it so that they view themselves as "born to be bad"; this is particularly likely if the child has LOW SELF-ESTEEM
- **Personality Differences:** Children who are NEUROTIC-EXTRAVERTS will not respond to CONDITIONING and will pick up NEGATIVE LABELS more easily than positive ones (SFP rather than SDP)

The most influential theory of development is SOCIAL LEARNING THEORY (SLT; **Bandura, 1977**). Based on Bandura's 'Bobo Doll' experiments in the 1960s, SLT proposes that:

- Children learn by OBSERVATION
- They observe MODELS and imitate what they see the models do
- Models are influential if the child IDENTIFIES with them (e.g. same sex) and they have STATUS in the child's eyes (e.g. an adult); **Bandura et al., 1961**
- Models on film/TV are just as influential as real-life models (**Bandura et al., 1963**)
- Children are more likely to imitate models who are seen to be rewarded (VICARIOUS REINFORCEMENT; **Bandura et al., 1965**)

*You studied all 3 of the 'Bobo Doll' studies as part of the **Learning Approach** in Unit 1. Now is a good time to revise these.*

Bandura proposes 4 MEDIATIONAL PROCESSES going on in the mind of an observer that affects how likely imitation is. These are summed up as **A.R.R.M.**:

1. **Attention**: How much attention do we pay to the behaviour? Do we notice it or ignore it? Is it ubiquitous (going on all around us) or drawn to our attention?
2. **Retention**: How well is the behaviour remembered?
3. **Reproduction**: Is it possible for us to imitate the behaviour? Children observe things they are not able to reproduce (lacking strength, money or social skills)
4. **Motivation**: Do we have an incentive to perform the behaviour? This boils down to a COST-BENEFIT ANALYSIS: will we gain more than we lose by acting in this way? This is why VICARIOUS REINFORCEMENT is important, because if we see others being rewarded we assume we will be rewarded too.

Since children's TV presents heroes (usually male) who use violence to win and are rewarded for it (e.g. superheroes, ninja turtles, power rangers), this explains why young boys develop differently from young girls. These expectations are SOCIAL SCRIPTS. This is why Bandura found boys and girls equally likely to imitate verbal aggression, but the boys were much more likely to imitate physical aggression. There are concerns that ONLINE PORNOGRAPHY models abusive behaviour towards women that is imitated by young boys.

By depicting women as men's willing sexual playthings, porn contributes to rape – **Andrea Dworkin**

EVALUATING INDIVIDUAL DIFFERENCES IN CRIME AO3

Credibility

Individual differences like personality and gender 'bridge the gap' between biological and social explanations. They offer an INTERACTIONIST explanation: biology and environment shape personality, but personality can overrule our biology and environment.

Developmental perspectives (like Social Learning Theory) show how we learn offending behaviour at an early age from observing adults, TV, film and video games despite the best efforts of parents and teachers to provide different messages. Personality suggests why some children learn from antisocial role models and labelling but others don't.

Weaknesses

Personality types can be very vague. **Extraversion** seems to involve confidence (which is a good thing) and thrill-seeking (which can be a problem). **Psychoticism** involves egotism and selfishness (bad) but also artistic creativity (good). Many researchers think Eysenck's terms should be defined more carefully and split into different sub-types.

Since **Eysenck** got his definition of P (Psychoticism) from studying criminals, it seems more like a description of what criminals are like than an explanation of why they do crimes. For example, murderers are cold-hearted people, but that doesn't explain why they chose to murder someone rather than deal with their problems in a better way.

Hare's definition of **psychopathy** can be positive if you're a salesman (charming and manipulative), a paramedic (not squeamish) or a soldier (prepared to kill people). It's not a good explanation of criminality if the same traits are found in law-abiding people.

SLT explains how children imitate antisocial behaviour but not where such behaviour comes from in the first place (someone must have started it off without imitating). Also, some offending behaviours (such as fraud) are not imitated from TV or video games.

Applications

Using psychometric tests like the EPQ and PCL can identify offenders who are strongly psychotic or psychopathic. This can help work out whether judges should set a custodial (prison) sentence and whether prisons should let offenders out on parole (since these people are likely to re-offend and break parole if let out).

However, there are issues of human rights and freewill at stake. It's wrong to lock someone up and refuse them parole simply because they scored badly on a questionnaire. Psychopaths, psychotics and neurotic-extraverts have freewill and can choose to stop offending, just like anyone else, and should not be discriminated against.

SLT suggests we should protect children from TV violence, video games that glamorise gangsterism and (a big concern) online pornography that encourages sex offending.

FURTHER REFLECTIONS

> *You could be set a 16-mark essay question on any of the 'explanations of crime'. Since there could be up to 10 marks for AO3, so you should try to go beyond the basic evaluation points.*

Psychological explanations of crime are part of the NATURE-NURTURE DEBATE. One view is that criminals are 'born that way' with something in their nature that drives them to offend. This is often the view of the Biological Approach with its focus on brains and genes. This sort of explanation tends to 'demonize' offenders by presenting them as monstrous and alien (*"moral strangers"*) and having no FREEWILL.

In turn, this view often leads to calls for harsh sentencing (since offenders are monsters, there's nothing to be done with them except locking them up or even executing them).

> *Politically, this view of crime is linked to right-wing parties who often support tough policing and prison as a punishment. In the USA it is sometimes used to support the death penalty.*

Many biological psychologists resist these simplistic conclusions. In his classic study of murderers' brains, **Adrian Raine** goes out of his way to argue that his results do *not* show that the murderers couldn't tell right from wrong, had no freewill or were 'born that way'. Other researchers emphasise that biology only gives people PREDISPOSITIONS and that other factors will influence whether or not they act on their biology.

The other view is the 'society creates criminals' through bad upbringing, tough environments, poor role models and biased policing. This is the view of the Social Approach with its focus on labelling and social learning. This explanation tends to condemn society for its unfairness rather than offenders for their badness (although it still downplays freewill on the part of criminals, suggesting 'society made them do it').

This view often leads to calls for more lenient sentencing (since offenders are unlucky people and anyone put into their situation would do the same things).

> *Politically, this view of crime is linked to left-wing parties who often support non-custodial sentences (keeping offenders out of prison) and gentler policing strategies.*

Personality theories have a bigger focus on freewill: offenders **choose** to offend because they crave excitement or are moody or lack empathy or are selfish. Psychopaths get a delight out of cheating or dominating other people. However, these theories also relate to nature/nurture because we want to know where personality *comes from*. **Eysenck** argues personality is 75% nature and only 25% nurture; research into psychopathy suggests it is a brain disorder that has a genetic basis.

The INTERACTIONIST view tries to 'split the difference' by saying that nature and nurture share equal responsibility for crime. A good upbringing will steer a psychopath away from crime but a bad upbringing might make a criminal out of a normal person.

REVISING EXPLANATIONS OF CRIME

DEFINITIONS
AMYGDALA
ARRM
BRUNNER SYNDROME
CSDD
EMPATHY
EPQ
fMRI
GENE
MONOAMINE OXIDASE-A
PCL
PEN MODEL
PREDISPOSITION
SDP
SFP
SLT
SURVIVAL TRAIT
XYY SYNDROME

RESEARCH SUMMARIES
BESEMER *ET AL.* (2013)
BLAIR *ET AL.* (1996)
BRUNNER *ET AL.* (1993)
EYSENCK (1966)
FARRINGTON *ET AL.* (1982)
GLENN *ET AL.* (2009)
JAHODA (1954)
ROSENTHAL & JACOBSON (1968)
TILHONEN *ET AL.* (2015)
WITKIN (1976)
YANG *ET AL.* (2009)

RESEARCH
Find out more about recent trends in crime in the UK
(tip: use the **bbb.co.uk site** to search for 'crime statistics)
- What types of crime are increasing or decreasing?
- Are male and female crime rates converging?
- What age groups commit crime?

COMPREHENSION QUESTIONS
1. What was Lombroso's explanation of crime?
2. How does the 'Warrior Gene' cause crime?
3. What is the argument against linking XYY Syndrome to crime?
4. What is the role of the amygdala in crime?
5. What is the difference between retrospective and projective labelling?
6. What is a master status label?
7. Why is self-esteem important for labelling?
8. How do males and females score differently on the EPQ?
9. What are the problems with Eysenck's definition of Psychoticism?
10. What is a psychopath?
11. What are social scripts?
12. What is an interactionist view of crime?

EXAM-STYLE QUESTIONS

Darren is big for his age and has learning difficulties. Because of this, teachers and neighbours assume he will become a thug, especially since his father has been to prison.

(a) State the meaning of XYY Syndrome. [2 marks AO1]

(b) Explain possible effects of labelling on Darren. [4 marks AO2]

(c) To what extent does criminality have a biological explanation? [8 marks AO1+AO3]

UNDERSTANDING THE OFFENDER

A FORENSIC PSYCHOLOGIST assists the police with offender profiling, gives evidence in court and advises parole boards and mental health tribunals. They also help to treat prisoners (such as anger management or drug rehab). Commonly, a forensic psychologist carries out one-to-one interviews to assess the risk of self-harm, suicide or re-offending (e.g. for lifers being released into the community or sex offenders after treatment).

If this career interests you, you will need a 3-year degree in Psychology, membership of the British Psychological Society (BPS) and then a post-graduate qualification like a 1-year Masters or the BPS' own qualification in Forensic Psychology

OFFENCE ANALYSIS

A Forensic Psychologist analyses the crime and the offender to work out the chance of RECIDIVISM (which is repeating the offending behaviour after being treated or punished).

The main framework for this in the UK is OFFENCE PARALLELING BEHAVIOUR (OPB), developed by **Lawrence Jones (1997)**. Offenders have consistent reactions to things that produce a pattern in their behaviour. Although these reactions might look different because they occur in different situations (they are TOPOGRAPHICALLY different), they have the same reason behind them (they are FUNCTIONALLY similar).

Jones (2010) gives the example of a rapist who is humiliated by a mistake at work: sexual attack makes him feel powerful instead. In prison, he experiences similar humiliation but cannot respond by offending so instead he is verbally aggressive to the therapist; he later fantasizes about offending against her. Aggression and fantasy serves the same FUNCTION as offending: humiliation is replaced by feeling powerful.

OPB involves identifying CONTINGENCIES (circumstances) that trigger offending. This can be humiliation (in the example above) or things like drinking alcohol, taking drugs, being with certain friends or going to certain places. These contingencies are CRIMOGENIC: they cause criminal behaviour.

Jones also considers that crime is an ADDICTIVE BEHAVIOUR in its own right and follows the pattern found with drug addiction:

- **Salience:** Offending is pleasurable and gives a feeling of power and control
- **Tolerance:** Offenders need to escalate their offending to get the same thrill
- **Withdrawal:** They experience distress if they go without offending
- **Conflict:** Offending creates problems in family, relationships and work (ultimately, going to prison)
- **Relapse:** After a period of resistance, offenders might go back to their offending behaviour

Jack Katz (*The Seductions of Crime,* **1988**) argues that crime is pleasurable: Katz describes the *"sneaky thrills"* of shoplifting, the *"righteous slaughter"* of murder and the robber's feeling that he has *"succeeded in making a fool of his victim"*. Katz argues males in particular are attracted to the chaos, thrill and danger of crime as a solution to boredom and powerlessness.

OPB uses the YOUNG SCHEMA MODEL developed by **Jeffrey Young (2003)**. This is the idea that people interpret the world and organize their memories using SCHEMAS.

> *You studied Schema Theory as part of **Cognitive Psychology** in Unit 1, so now is a good time to revise it.*

Young proposes that offenders have UNMET EMOTIONAL NEEDS from childhood that lead them to develop EARLY MALADAPTIVE SCHEMAS (EMS): perceptions of themselves and their memories which are 'maladaptive' because they are trying to cope with problems in ways that only create more problems.

For example, someone who was abandoned as a child develops an **'Abandonment Schema'**. They perceive abandonment in ordinary behaviour (such as someone not returning a phone call) and exaggerate abandonment in their memories while forgetting episodes of friendship and support. This might explain STALKING BEHAVIOUR when an ex-partner (or total stranger online) becomes sexually obsessed with a victim.

- **Avoidance:** This is avoiding contingencies (situations) that activate the schema; this can be maladaptive if it ruins your life (such as never forming relationships)
- **Overcompensation:** This is working hard to prevent the schema from happening; it can be maladaptive since it leads to fear and anxiety and reinforces the schema
- **Surrender:** This is 'giving in' to the schema and basing your life on it; this is always maladaptive and it also reinforces the schema.

The **Young Schema Questionnaire (YSQ)** features 232 questions about self-image, rated from 1 (*completely untrue of me*) to 6 (*describes me perfectly*). The results fit the respondent into 18 possible maladaptive schemas (e.g. abandonment, shame, abuse).

> *You can view some of the questions at **http://www.schematherapy.com/id53.htm***

CASE FORMULATION

Offence Analysis and techniques like OPB don't just help with assessing offenders for **recidivism**; they also help with **offender treatment**. This is CASE FORMULATION.

- **OPB** reveals how offending is FUNCTIONAL for a criminal: the behaviour serves a purpose or feeds a psychological need.
- The **Young Schema Model** focuses on the underlying SCHEMA that drives offending behaviour

Case formulation can provide recommendations for:

- **Clinical psychologists** providing counseling for offenders
- **Judges or parole boards** deciding whether an offender should be released

OPB is based on cognitive psychology, but there are other approaches:

- **Behavioural approach:** Using the **operant conditioning** theory of **Skinner**, this case formulation focuses on **reinforcement** and **punishment** rather than schemas and functions; it is more based on environmental stimuli than beliefs and recommends **Token Economy Programmes (TEPs).**
- **Psychodynamic approach:** Using the psychodynamic theories of **Freud**, this focuses on **unconscious desires** and **defence mechanisms**; it is based on beliefs rather than environmental stimuli but proposes that offenders cannot know their own unconscious thoughts without PSYCHOANAYSIS to help them

> *You studied Psychodynamic Theory as part of the **Biological Approach** and operant conditioning as part of the **Learning Approach** so you should revise these now.*

Paul Whitehead et al. (2007, *c.f.* p33 also**)** provide a case study of **Mr C**, a 28-year-old Maori from New Zealand with 20 convictions for burglary and violence. Mr C is a gang-member with tattoos that show his gang loyalty.

- Mr C experienced childhood violence and sexual abuse and went to live with his grandfather to escape this
- He was a school bully, frequently truanted and left school at 15 without qualifications; this was when he joined criminal gangs (which included some family members) and began using weapons
- As a teenager he lived with prostitutes, was sexually assaulted himself and sexually assaulted women

Case formulation for Mr C might take a variety of approaches:

- **Contingencies:** Mr C offends when around his gang and family members
- **Schemas:** Mr C associates power with physical violence; he understands sex in terms of dominance; he **surrenders** to these schemas
- **Social Learning Theory (SLT):** Mr C's **role models** in his family and gang are violent and sexually abusive
- **Behavioural:** Mr C's violence is **positively reinforced** by approval from the gang and **negatively reinforced** by preventing him from being victimized again
- **Psychodynamic:** Mr C is in **denial** about his own suffering and vulnerability; he **projects** his own pain onto other people as abuses them the way he was abused

Whitehead focuses on SLT case formulation and recommends the GOOD LIVES MODEL of **offender treatment** (p33).

EVALUATING UNDERSTANDING THE OFFENDER AO3

Credibility

Jones' OPB FRAMEWORK has been widely adopted by forensic psychologists. The idea is that although a prison or hospital is TOPOGRAPHICALLY different from the outside world, it is possible to observe behaviour that is FUNCTIONALLY similar in prisoners.

Stephen Hart (2011) suggests case formulations can be evaluated based on COHERENCE (does it fit established psychological theories?), DIACHRONICITY (does it explain the past and predict the future?), SIMPLICITY (does it boil explanations down to simple problems?) and GENERATIVITY (does it produce predictions about what offenders will do that can be tested?).

Kadra *et al.* (2014) found OPB very successful in predicting outcomes for 5 violent offenders in a UK secure psychiatric unit compared to randomly assigned predictions (however, note the small sample size). This shows **diachronicity** and **generativity**.

Weaknesses

Sturmley & McMurren (2011) point out a lack of empirical evidence for the success of OPB. Very important decisions hang upon case formulation (such as whether or not to release a violent offender on parole) and if OPB focuses on the wrong behaviours and contingencies, the public may be at risk. The main criticism here is the SIMPLICITY of OPB, which focuses so much on particular schemas it can miss other factors.

Differences

As a cognitive approach, OPB assumes all behaviour comes from mental states (schemas, memories and self-image). Whitehead *et al.* (2007) argue for case formulation based more on SOCIAL LEARNING THEORY (SLT). OPB ignores **learned behaviour** and **role models** and therapies based **token economy programmes**.

Applications

By focusing on behaviour in prisons and hospitals that is FUNCTIONALLY similar to offending behaviour, OPB helps evaluate whether offender treatment programmes are working. This could be particularly useful for identifying prisoners at risk or self-harm or suicide or dealing with PSYCHOPATHS who can fool normal interviews and observations. It's also useful for assessing sex offenders who may seem harmless in a prison or hospital where they have no opportunity to offend the way they do outside.

Atkinson & Mann (2011) suggest training prison officers in OPB so that they can contribute their insights into case formulation. This is good because prison officers have more daily contact with prisoners than forensic psychologists, but it risks spoiling the relationship between officers and prisoners if the staff are viewed as 'spying' on them.

TREATMENTS FOR OFFENDERS

The Edexcel Specification expects you to learn about:

- **Cognitive-behavioural treatment:** CBT focuses on the offender's faulty thinking (such as **maladaptive schemas**) and uses **counselling** to replace faulty thoughts with healthy ones
- **Biological treatment:** this either uses drugs or surgical procedures to alter brain chemistry or else alters neurology more indirectly through diet or exercise

COGNITIVE-BEHAVIOURAL: THE GOOD LIVES MODEL (WARD, 2002)

The GOOD LIVES MODEL (GLM) was developed by New Zealand psychologist **Tony Ward** and is being tested in Australia and Canada. GLM recognises that all human beings have similar goals in life, and that offending is a confused attempt to reach these goals:

- Health and physical safety
- Relationships and friendships
- Peace of mind
- Happiness/pleasure
- Being part of a group
- Creativity
- Being good at what we do (work or hobbies)
- Learning about things that interest us
- Independence (i.e. being in control of our lives)

Offending behaviour is a 'short-cut' to get to these life goals when there are obstacles in the way. These short-cuts offer immediate satisfaction but lead to long-term problems for other people and eventually the offender too. For example, someone who is having relationship problems might turn to violence as a short-cut to hold onto a relationship: there is a brief sense of satisfaction for the offender but long-term misery for everyone.

GLM helps offenders identify what they *want* their life to look like and how to get there without harming themselves or others. This involves identifying what your life goals actually are, noticing how your past behaviour was an unsatisfying short-cut towards these goals and deciding on future behaviour that will achieve these goals in a more satisfying and less harmful way. Ward calls this a *"strength-based approach"* because it encourages offenders to work towards personally meaningful goals and to see themselves as having the skills and resources to fulfil their life goals, rather than viewing themselves as failures who need help from other people.

It also goes against the tendency to **label** offenders as *"moral strangers"* with alien and unpleasant values (and create a SELF-FULFILLING PROPHECY) – it focuses on them as *"fellow travellers"* who fundamentally want the same 'Good Life' as everyone else.

The case study of **Mr C** by **Whitehead et al. (2007, p31)** describes his progress using GLM. The first quote is from Mr C in prison after 100 hours of standard CBT:

> *I'm in now, bro. Been here for about a week. First day here I smashed someone over... –* **Mr C**

The next quote is after GLM treatment with a Maori counsellor focusing on Mr C's need for friendship and feelings of control to have a 'good life':

> *To change my life I need to change the way I think and live... I'm given a chance to start a new life and a new way of living –* **Mr C**

Mr C's 'good life' involved going to university (the first member of his family to do this), having a steady relationship and taking up a hobby (diving).

After leaving prison, Mr C was reviewed at 14 months and only had a minor driving offence on his record. He admitted to using violence on two occasions (after being knocked over at a party and when his partner was insulted); this made him feel ashamed and want to join his gang again, but he *"activated his safety plan"* and contacted his mentor instead. This is a dramatic turn-around in lifestyle and attitude.

Strengths	Weaknesses
Focus on OFFENDER AGENCY – putting the offender in charge of their own life	Depends on PERSONAL RELATIONSHIP with counsellor
Focus on offender's PERSONAL VALUES – their own personal code	Introduces SUBJECTIVE BIAS into case formulation
Creates a LIFE PLAN that focuses on more than just not being arrested again	EXTERNAL OBSTACLES to a 'Good Life' e.g. poverty, racism, isolation
HOLISTIC (non-reductionist) approach that covers all aspects of life	Ignores possibility offenders are MORAL STRANGERS (e.g. psychopaths)

BIOLOGICAL: DIET-BASED OFFENDER TREATMENT (GESCH, 2002)

Another unusual approach to offender treatment involves diet. This has been championed by Oxford scientist **Bernard Gesch**. Gesch argues that much antisocial behaviour is explained by poor diet, in particular a lack of vitamins, minerals and essential fatty acids.

> *It may seem a little strange that what we eat has got anything to do with criminal justice. This is potentially something that is very simple, very humane. It is likely to be very cheap and it has been largely overlooked –* **Bernard Gesch**

The biology behind this is that behavioural problems, especially violence, have been linked to deficiencies in **omega 3 fatty acids** (e.g. **Meyer et al., 2013**). Omega-3 (found in fish oil) is essential for a healthy brain. Low levels of **magnesium** and **zinc** are linked with **hyperactive** behaviour and impaired **brain development** (e.g. **Villagomez, 2014**)

Gesch et al. (2002) carried out the 'Aylesbury Study' in the 1990s. The researchers tested 231 violent young offenders (aged 18-21) who took diet supplement pills for between 2 weeks and 9 months.

Half took pills containing omega-3 fatty acids and half were a PLACEBO group (vegetable oil pills with no nutritional value). The two types of pill look and taste the same.

The young offenders taking the real diet supplements showed a 26% drop in offences over the period and a 37% drop in violent offences. The placebo group did not change.

Zaalberg et al. (2010) replicated Gesch's study in the Netherlands with 221 young offenders (age 18-25) over 3 months. This Dutch study used more omega-3 and magnesium in the supplements than Gesch did. Violent incidents dropped 34% for the experimental group (similar to Gesch) but actually *increased* by 14% for the placebo group. This was a DOUBLE-BLIND design (neither prisoners nor staff knew which prisoners were taking omega-3 and which were taking placebos). Zaalberg also used questionnaires to measure personality and cognitions (e.g. impulsivity, empathy) and found no change in these scores— so behaviour improved but cognitions didn't.

> *Does this means that the questionnaires are no good? Or is it just that behaviour changes quickly but it takes longer for personality and thought processes to 'catch up' with changed behaviour?*

Emily Deans (2017) explains these results by pointing out a huge change in our diets over the last 40 years, replacing OMEGA-3 in our diets (seafood, animal fat like lard) with highly processed vegetable oils (e.g. sunflower oil).

> *What do I conclude from a common-sense analysis of the massive change in our diets coupled with a knowledge of how omega 3s are important for our neurons? Our brains seem to be designed to run on fish oil* – **Emily Deans**

UK prisons are committed to providing a healthy diet and avoiding processed food, but have to do this on a budget of £1.96 per prisoner per day (source: **National Offender Management Service, 2014**). However, prisoners can buy junk food (sweets, biscuits, pot noodles, fizzy drinks) from the 'canteen' (prison shop) and tend to avoid healthy foods like salads, baked potatoes and pasta provided by the prison kitchens.

Strengths	Weaknesses
CHEAP: diet supplements are much cheaper than professional counsellors	REDUCTIONIST: ignores personality, values, thought processes and choice
HEALTH BENEFITS go beyond behaviour, such as reduced heart disease	Does not prevent RECIDIVISM if diet supplements are not taken outside prison
CONSTRUCT VALIDITY: ties in with advice from nutritionists for children	UNETHICAL to impose diet supplements without consent
SAFETY: reducing violence in prisons makes staff and other prisoners safer	Not GENERALISABLE to non-violent offending (e.g. theft, fraud)

EVALUATING OFFENDER TREATMENT PROGRAMMES AO3

Credibility

Research supporting the GOOD LIVES MODEL is in short supply, although it is increasing as more prisons try it out. Usually, GLM is put in place alongside established COGNITIVE BEHAVIOURAL THERAPY (CBT) and seems to make CBT more effective. In particular, GLM helps offenders pursue positive life goals when they leave prison.

The research linking poor diet to behavioural problems is immense. Back in the 19th century, **Cesare Lombroso (1892, p8)** explained bomb-throwing anarchists by their corn-heavy diet. **Adrian Raine** is currently researching the positive effects of OMEGA-3 on the brain: **Raine *et al.* (2015)** studied American 12-year-olds with behavioural problems and found an omega-3 supplement alongside CBT reduced violence more than CBT alone.

Weaknesses

Because GLM is usually run alongside standard CBT, it's difficult to be sure where the benefit is coming from. The case study of Mr C shows a change in the offender's attitude after GLM, but perhaps it merely took time for the effects of the original CBT to 'sink in'.

The case study by **Whitehead *et al.*** cannot be generalised because Mr C could be an unusual prisoner whose desire to 'turn his life around' might not be typical of offenders. **Tony Ward** developed GLM after researching New Zealand Maori offenders like Mr C. The Maori have a warrior-culture and GLM seems to appeal to a masculine code of honour, but might be less successful with other types of offenders (e.g. women, criminals who aren't in gangs) and in other cultures.

Diet studies suffer from the problem that researchers cannot be sure that prisoners are really taking their pills. However, more recent studies (like Adrian Raine's) use blood tests to check levels of minerals and omega-3.

All offender treatments require the offenders to **want** to take part, which means the sample is skewed in favour of the more helpful prisoners. Bernard Gesh could not persuade the Aylesbury prisoners to participate until he approached *"the biggest, toughest guy around"* and persuaded him to take the pills and get the other prisoners to join in: this is a SNOWBALL SAMPLE which might not be representative of even that prison, never mind prisoners generally.

Differences

There's a huge contrast between treatments that tackle the mind (like GLM) and those that tackle the body (like diet). Cognitive-behavioural therapies try to turn around the whole person by giving the offender a different way of looking at their problems and a different way of getting what they want out of life. If they are successful, they bring about PERSONAL TRANSFORMATION, turning an angry and confused troublemaker into someone who can be a responsible citizen, employee, partner and parent. This has huge knock-on effects for everyone connected to the offender who will have more positive relationships with them.

By contrast, diet alters the offender's body chemistry without them realising and brings about behavioural changes without them noticing (which is perhaps why they didn't show any personality changes in the Dutch prison diet study). If the diet stops (such as when they leave prison), they will probably go straight back to offending. Nonetheless, improved diet makes prisoners much more manageable while they are in prison.

Applications

There are several campaigns to improve prison diet, such as Bernard Gesh's NATURAL JUSTICE (since 1991) and Lucy Vincent's FOOD BEHIND BARS (since 2016). Vincent goes into prisons to advise staff on recipes and run workshops with prisoners, teaching them cooking skills they can use on the outside.

> *the majority of people in prison come from quite deprived socioeconomic backgrounds, where things like healthy eating have never featured into their lives before* – **Lucy Vincent**

Gesh's diet supplement would cost £4 million to roll out across al prisons – which sounds a lot but the total UK prison budget is over £4 billion (source: **Statistica, 2018**).

In 2013, the Scottish Government launched a MOVING FORWARD, MAKING CHANGES (MFMC) programme, based on GLM, for use with sex offenders. Sex-offenders benefit from a therapy that does not see them as MORAL STRANGERS and helps them find healthy and non-abusive sexual relationships. However, *The Scottish Sun* **(2015)** revealed a 6-month waiting list for the *"Fiends' therapy"* (as they called it) due to budget cuts. Words like 'fiend' and 'pervert' shows that sex offenders are still seen as *moral strangers*.

REVISING UNDERSTANDING/TREATING THE OFFENDER

DEFINITIONS
CASE FORMULATION
CBT
CONTINGENCIES
CRIMOGENIC
DOUBLE-BLIND
GLM
LIFE GOALS
MALADAPTIVE SCHEMAS
OFFENCE ANALYSIS
OMEGA-3
OPB
PLACEBO
YSQ

RESEARCH SUMMARIES
GESH *ET AL.* (2002)
JONES (2010)
KADRA *ET AL.* (2014)
RAINE *ET AL.* (2015)
WHITEHEAD *ET AL.* (2007)
ZAALBERG *ET AL.* (2010)

COMPREHENSION QUESTIONS
1. What is the job of a forensic psychologist?
2. How can offending be functionally similar but topographically different?
3. How is offending like addiction?
4. How can unmet emotional needs lead to offending?
5. What is an Abandonment Schema?
6. Why is GLM a *"strength-based"* treatment?
7. Why are offenders treated like *"moral strangers"* and why is this bad?
8. Why is omega-3 important for diet?
9. Why are placebo groups important?
10. Why do prisoners often have bad diets?
11. What does Food Behind Bars aim to do?
12. What problems has the Scottish MFMC programme run into?

RESEARCH
Research a profile of a famous criminal and create your own case formulation.
https://www.crimemuseum.org/crime-library/serial-killers/
- What is the offender's background?
- Identify contingencies, maladaptive schemes and 'short cut' life goals

EXAM-STYLE QUESTIONS

Vincent is a 20-year-old young offender with a history of violence and gang membership. He comes from an abusive home background and continues to be violent in prison. The prison governor would like to use a cognitive-behavioural therapy on Vincent but the forensic psychologist would like to try a biological treatment.

(a) State the meaning of cognitive-behavioural therapy. [2 marks AO1]

(b) Explain one strength and one weakness of biological treatments for offenders. [4 marks AO3]

(c) Using your knowledge of Psychology, explain how EITHER a cognitive-behavioural treatment OR a biological treatment could help Vincent. [8 marks AO1+AO2]

EYEWITNESS TESTIMONY

EYEWITNESS TESTIMONY (EWT) is refers to **the description of an event given by people who observed it**. As a legal term, it usually refers to **the report by witnesses to a crime, made to the police and repeated in court**. It might include identifying an offender, describing a crime scene or the victim reporting the crime itself.

EWT is immensely important: police use it to identify the suspect they charge with a crime and juries are very influenced by eyewitnesses when it comes to passing a verdict of 'innocent' or 'guilty'. However, EWT has been shown to be UNRELIABLE (when details are recalled incorrectly and the wrong suspect is identified).

> *You studied 4 theories of memory as part of Cognitive Psychology in **Unit 1**: the **Multistore Model, Working Memory, Long Term Memory** and **Reconstructive Memory** (Schema Theory). You should revise these as part of this topic.*

Police ask eyewitnesses to identify suspects with several procedures:

- **Line-up:** The suspect and four or five "FOILS" (similar-looking people) are observed, usually through a one-way mirror. The eyewitness identifies the person they recognise. It's important to advise the eyewitness that the offender might not be in the lineup, otherwise the eyewitness might identify someone who *just looks most-similar* to the offender.
- **Mugshots:** The witness looks through a gallery of head-and-shoulder photographs of previously-arrested suspects and identifies the person they recognise. As above, the witness must be warned that the offender may not be in the gallery and there is a danger of some faces standing out (e.g. colour of background)
- **Facial composites:** This involves building up a face 'jigsaw-style' from illustrates of chins, mouths, noses, eyes, etc. The original **Identikit** (1959) used drawings of facial features, but it was replaced by **PhotoFit** (1970, photographs) and modern **E-FIT** (1980s, a computer database of features).
- **Police artist:** The preferred method of the FBI is to use a sketch artist to draw the face based on the witness' description. The **EFIT-V** computer program imitates this process by generating random faces that gradually 'morph' into a final image based on the witness' descriptions

There is a debate about whether line-ups should be SIMULTANEOUS (the suspect and foils together at once) or SEQUENTIAL (viewing each person separately then making a decision at the end). **Gary Wells *et al.* (2014)** shows that sequential line-ups produce more conservative judgements: witnesses are less likely to make a positive identification but they also make fewer false identifications. Nonetheless, simultaneous line-ups are more common.

Thee is another debate about whether facial composites reflect the way we actually remember faces. Research by **Vicki Bruce *et al.* (1999)** suggests people use EXTERNAL FEATURES (chin, hair, shape of face) to recall and recognise faces, but are poor at using INTERNAL FEATURES (mouth, nose, eyes): Bruce asked students to recognise famous celebrities but found the success rate was only 24% if they were shown internal features (slightly above chance) compared to 42% for external features.

The GESTALT APPROACH to cognitive psychology suggests we remember faces 'as a whole' rather than as a collection of features. Police sketch artists come closer to this *Gestalt* way of remembering as does the EFIT-V system.

RELIABILITY OF EWT

In 1975 an Australian psychologist, **Donald M. Thomson**, was invited to discuss the psychology of EWT on live TV. The next day, Thomson was picked up by local police. He was told that last night a woman was raped in her apartment and had named Thomson as her attacker. Thomson had a watertight alibi. He had been on TV at the time of the attack and in the presence of the assistant commissioner of police. The victim had been watching Thomson on TV and had ***confused his face with that of her attacker***.

When a person recollects something and inserts it into a current thought without realizing where it really came from, this is CRYPTOMNESIA.

> *If a friend tells you some exciting news, forgetting that you were the one who told them in the first place, but insists they "just came up with it" or "saw it on TV", that would be **cryptomnsesia** too.*

Donald Thompson was released but many others have not been so lucky. **Gary Wells** identified 40 different US miscarriages of justice that relied on faulty EWT (**Wells *et al.*, 1998**). For example, **Ed Honaker** w had been convicted of rape on the basis of the victim's EWT; however, Honaker's mugshot had a different background from the other suspects, making it more likely to be picked out. DNA evidence later confirmed Honaker's innocence and he was released in 1994 after serving 10 years in a US prison.

- The **contemporary study** by **Valentine & Mesout (2009)** examines how stress affects the reliability of EWT.

POST-EVENT INFORMATION

An important factor in the reliability of EWT is information received after the event that causes witnesses to change how they recall things.

Fiona Gabbert *et al.* (2003) tested 60 students and 60 older adults in Aberdeen, Scotland. Participants watched a video of a girl stealing money from a wallet then completed a **questionnaire** about what they recalled:

- **CONTROLS:** These participants recalled details alone
- **CO-WITNESS:** These participants were paired and discussed the video together before responding. They were told they had watched the same video, but in reality had seen different films, with only one showing the theft itself.

71% of the co-witnesses recalled information they had not actually seen (60% said that the girl was guilty, despite not seeing her commit the crime). This shows how post-event information (from discussion with another witness) affects EWT.

In Gabbert's study the post-event information was true (the girl **was** guilty) but it still produced a FALSE MEMORY. **Elizabeth Loftus** calls this the MISINFORMATION EFFECT.

> *The misinformation effect refers to the impairment in memory for the past that arises after exposure to misleading information* – **Elizabeth Loftus**

- The **classic study** by **Loftus & Palmer (1974**, p87**)** examines post-event information and EWT.

Several factors add to the misinformation effect:

- **Time:** The bigger the gap between the original event and the misleading information, the more likely the memory is to become distorted.
- **Discussion with other witnesses:** The recollections other witnesses can conflict with the original memory, distorting the witness's original memory of events.
- **News reports:** Reading news stories and watching TV reports leads people to mistakenly believe that they personally observed things they saw in the news.
- **Repeated exposure:** The more often people are exposed to misleading information, the more likely memory is to become distorted.

The misinformation effect can be explained by the theory of RECONSTRUCTIVE MEMORY. We create memories using SCHEMAS to 'fill in the blanks' but we are very poor at telling which details from a memory are genuine and which are CONFABULATED.

> *You studied **Reconstructive Memory** and **Schemas** as part of the Cognitive Approach in **Unit 1**. You should revise it now.*

Loftus & Pickrell (1995) demonstrate this with their famous 'Lost in the Mall' study. 24 participants were presented with 4 stories about their own childhood (provided by an older relative) but the 3rd was always a false account of becoming lost in the shopping mall at age 5. 5 (26%) of the participants recalled this as a real memory.

Kimberley Wade *et al.* (2002) replicates this, replacing 'lost in the mall' with a false account of taking a flight in a hot air balloon, using doctored childhood photographs. 10 (50%) of the participants recalled this as a real memory after this extra level of misinformation.

WEAPON FOCUS (Loftus, Loftus & Messo, 1987)

Elizabeth Loftus and her then-husband Geoffrey Loftus investigated how, during a crime, a witness' attention focuses on the weapon at the expense of the offender's face. 36 students watched a slide show of 18 scenes in a fast-food restaurant. Each slide was shown for 1½ seconds.

- **CONTROLS:** The slides showed the second customer taking out their wallet
- **EXPERIMENTAL (WEAPON FOCUS):** The slides showed the second customer taking out a gun

The students' eye movements were monitored using an ELECTRO-OCULOGRAPH (EOG). They then completed a multiple choice questionnaire and picked the second customer out of a line-up of 12 head-and-shoulder photographs. Finally, they were asked to rate how confident they were about their selection, from 1 (guesswork) to 6 (total certainty).

There was no difference in answers to the questionnaire but the line-up produced different results. The chance of picking the out correct photo randomly was 8½%.

- In the **control group**, 38.9% chose the correct photo
- In the **experimental condition** only 11.1% got it right (barely above chance).

There was no difference in the confidence levels. EOG showed more eye focus on the gun than the wallet (significant at $p<0.025$).

Loftus suggests that the dangerous weapon is **arousing**, so we pay more attention to it. However, **Kerri Pickel (1999)** suggests that it is the **unusualness**, rather than the danger, that is distracting. Pickel showed students short videos about a man with a gun and they recalled details better if the setting was appropriate for guns (a rifle range, rather than a baseball game) or if the man was appropriate for guns (a police officer, rather than a priest). This suggests we remember things better that fit in with out SCHEMAS.

EVALUATING EYEWITNESS TESTIMONY AO3

Credibility

Unlike a lot of Criminological Psychology, EWT can be researched using well-designed **lab experiments** that look for the difference between **control and experimental conditions** on a **DV**. This sort of research reveals **cause-and-effect** (such as WEAPON FOCUS *causing* poor recognition of faces).

These experiments show how easily EWT can be distorted with very little pressure. When witnesses are in court, they face a lot of pressure during cross-examination from lawyers, so EWT in real life could be even more unreliable than these studies suggest.

Weaknesses

Lab experiments tend to be poor in **ecological validity**. Watching slides of a fictional robbery is not the same as being a real witness caught up in the surprise and alarm of a real crime. Photographs of guns are not as stressful as real guns.

Similarly, a lot more is at stake with real-life EWT: an innocent person might go to prison or an offender walk free. People might be more careless about false memories in a lab experiment than they would be in court or in front of the police.

Many of these studies involve university students, out of convenience. Students are not ideal for these types of studies because they tend to have superior recall (they are young and they exercise their memories through study) and they are statistically less likely to be a victim of or witness to a serious crime (being predominantly middle class and sheltered on secure campuses). Students may be prone to **demand characteristics** (Loftus is famous as a memory researcher specialising in misinformation and many of her students would know this).

Differences

There is a debate about how to explain these findings. Is it the case that witnesses simply do not recall crucial details and rely on post-event information in place of saying *"I don't remember"*? Or do SCHEMAS work by **actually changing our memories** into something different?

Similarly, do stress and arousal 'cloud' our memories when there are weapons present? Or do SCHEMAS make it hard for us to reconstruct memories of unusual events that don't 'fit in' with out expectations?

Applications

Loftus' research influenced the **Devlin Report** in the UK (**1976**) which instructed judges to warn all juries that EWT might be unreliable and even confident eyewitnesses could be mistaken. The Report recommended that no defendant should be convicted on the basis of a single unsupported eyewitness testimony. **C. Ronald Huff (1987)** concludes 300 out of 500 wrongful convictions (60%) were due to false EWT. **Wells & Bradfield (1998)** showed that DNA testing cleared 24 out of 28 convictions (86%) based on false EWT.

In the USA, Loftus herself often appears as an EXPERT WITNESS to advise juries about unreliable EWT. Loftus became involved in the case of **George Franklin**, who was accused by his own daughter of murdering her best friend a decade earlier. Franklin spent 5 yeas in prison but was released in 1996 when his daughter's testimony was shown to be a FALSE MEMORY implanted while receiving hypnosis therapy. The details she 'recalled' were all found in newspaper accounts of the unsolved murder. The fierce debate in the 1990s about false memories in court became known as the "MEMORY WARS".

POLICE INTERVIEWS

Standard police interview procedures can be ineffective: questions may be inappropriate, or poorly worded or sequenced; witnesses are often interrupted. **George & Clifford (1992)** report that, in the UK, police interviews have only a brief attempt to establish *rapport* (intimacy) followed by direct questions (*"Tell me what happened?"*) and a lot of interruptions (*"How tall was he?"*); many questions are LEADING QUESTIONS (*"He was wearing a red T-shirt, wasn't he?"*). The witness is very PASSIVE, waiting to answer questions and offering only brief replies.

THE COGNITIVE INTERVIEW (CI)

In 1991, two men murdered a worker in a Miami office building and the only witness was a woman who had passed the two attackers in the lobby. The police called in **Ron Fisher** to use his memory techniques. Fisher helped the witness recall one man brushing his hair from his face and the silver earring he was wearing. This proved to be a breakthrough in the case.

Edward Geiselman & Ron Fisher developed the COGNITIVE INTERVIEW (CI) to help police. It involves 4 techniques:

1. **Context Reinstatement:** The witness is asked to recreate the **context** of the incident in their mind, imagine themselves back at the scene along with any **emotional responses**. These feelings are as important for recall as remembering physical details about the place the event occurred in. The psychology behind this is the ENCODING SPECIFICITY HYPOTHESIS (**Tulving & Thompson, 1973**) which states that we recall better if we are in the same emotional state or physical place as when the memory was originally encoded.
2. **Focused retrieval:** The witness must recall *everything*, even trivial details. This is based on the HIERARCHICAL NETWORK MODEL (Collins & Quillian, 1969) which proposes that since memories form an interconnected network, if one CUE fails to retrieve a memory you can try a different cue.
3. **Extensive retrieval:** Witnesses put themselves in the place of other victims/witnesses; this **change of perspective** reduces the effects of SCHEMAS in producing false recall.
4. **Change Order:** Recalling events in an unusual order (starting in the middle, working backwards, etc.) may help witnesses recall things that don't fit in with SCHEMAS. This technique can disrupt **Context Reinstatement**, however.

An aim of CI is that 80% of the talking should be done by the witness, not the interviewer.

General features of CI are asking OPEN QUESTIONS (to encourage the witness to speak more), asking NEUTRAL QUESTIONS (that avoid the **misinformation effect**) and the FUNNEL APPROACH (where you start with a very broad question then narrow it with more specific follow-up questions based on the witness' responses).

Fisher *et al.* (1989) tested the CI in the field, with the help of 16 Miami police officers. The researchers recorded these detectives carrying out their **standard interviews** for 4 months (88 interviews), then split them into two groups:

- **CONTROLS:** 9 officers continued using standard techniques
- **EXPERIMENTAL (CI):** 7 detectives trained in CI techniques over 4 1-hour sessions

Over the next 7 months, interviews were recorded for both groups and analysed by a team at the University of California who were "blind" to the conditions (whether the detective was CI-trained or not).

The CI-trained detectives helped witnesses recall 47% more information than before their training (**repeated measures**) and 63% more than the untrained detectives (**independent groups**).

The interviews were checked for accuracy against another witness; of the 24 cases with this sort of corroborating evidence, 94% of the recalled information was corroborated.

Günter Köhnken *et al.* (1999) carried out a **meta-analysis** of 42 studies into CI (involving nearly 2500 interviews). They found a 34% increase in correct recall in CI compared to standard interviewing.

Milne & Bull (2002) tested the recall of children and university students with partial-CI. They found that each of the 4 techniques used by itself produced better recall than standard interviewing. They also found that **Context Reinstatement** and **Focused Retrieval** used together produced the best results.

ETHICAL INTERVIEWING TECHNIQUES

There are many ways that police interviewing can be unethical:

- **DECEPTION:** It's tempting to deceive suspects to get a confession (e.g. by telling them a witness has already identified them or their friends have accused them)
- **COERCION:** This is psychological pressure produced by intimidation, long periods of isolation, confusion about what's happening or threats about consequences (since police don't sentence offenders they should not threaten suspects with the type of punishment they will receive)
- **JUDGEMENTALISM:** Interviewers can have their minds made up about the suspect's guilt and question them in an unfair way

- **SHORT CUTS:** Police may be under pressure to get a confession and, by rushing the process, end up coercing the suspect or denying them their rights (e.g. to have a lawyer present)
- **SPECIAL NEEDS:** Many suspects have problems with mental health or substance abuse which need to be considered when interviewing them fairly; others may have poor English and need translators

John Baldwin (*Establishing Truth or Proof?* 1993) carried out a very influential review of police interview techniques in 6 British police stations in the late-1980s. He analysed 400 filmed interviews and 200 audio recordings. He was very critical of how suspects were interviewed.

- No *rapport* (trust, intimacy) is established
- **Assumption of guilt**: getting the suspect to accept the **police's version of events**
- **Interviewer doesn't listen** to suspect and **interrupts** the suspect's responses
- **Coercive:** an aggressive 'macho' approach to intimidate the suspect
- Interviews are **hurried** (one quarter taking only 10 minutes, most under 30 minutes and only 7% lasting more than an hour)

Photo: Dennis Crowley

Baldwin proposes that interviewing should be ETHICAL: police should build *RAPPORT* with suspects. Interviews should be NON-ACCUSATORY: police should focus on establishing **the truth of what happened** rather than just getting a confession of guilt.

Why do innocent people confess to crimes they haven't committed? **Gisli Gudjonsson (1992)** describes three types of FALSE CONFESSION:

- **Voluntary:** The innocent suspect confesses because they believe they are guilty (usually associated with mental disorders, e.g. schizophrenia)
- **Coerced-internalised:** The suspect is convinced by the police that they are guilty, although they are innocent (due to amnesia because of drugs or head injuries)
- **Coerced-compliant:** The person confesses though they know they are innocent (usually because of COERCIVE interrogation, the confession is a way out of the stressful situation)

To avoid these problems in future, the **Home Office** set of a group to propose better techniques for ethical interviewing and came up with the PEACE MODEL

P	Planning & Preparation
E	Engage & Explain
A	Account
C	Closure
E	Evaluate

Planning & Preparation
Lack of planning was a major criticism by Baldwin. Interviews should have clear objectives (not vague 'fishing trips' hoping that the suspect will offer up something of interest). The interviewer should study a profile of the interviewee beforehand.

Engage & Explain
Establishing *rapport* is important in interviews, instead of bullying. This means explain the purpose of the interview, setting fears to rest and making sure a suspect knows his or her legal rights (such as the presence of a lawyer). The interviewer sets the scene by explaining how important the interview is and that everything the interviewee says is important: they should not leave anything out, even if they believe it is of no relevance. The interviewee must be encouraged to ask questions if there is something they do not understand or do not know.

Account
Good questioning and listening skills are needed to produce a reliable Account. For cooperative interviewees (victims and witnesses), the COGNITIVE INTERVIEW (CI) technique could be used. For uncooperative interviewees, the interviewer might need to challenge the interviewee's Account. This "Challenge Phase" might focus on challenges to inconsistencies in the Account. Information may be held back for pre-planned challenges but interviewers must not use false information or deception to get a confession.

Closure
The interviewee needs to understand what has happened during the interview and it is important to explain what will happen next. A positive Closure keeps a good *rapport* and this means an interviewee will give any new information in the future. The Closure might help future interviews with other interviewees (through good 'word of mouth').

Evaluate
It's important to compare the interview with the objectives to see if it went as planned and learn from any mistakes. This involves reflecting on the information gathered and on whether the suspect was treated fairly.

EVALUATING POLICE INTERVIEWS AO3

Credibility

The COGNITIVE INTERVIEW (CI) is based on well-established theories of memory (**Encoding Specificity, Hierarchical Networks** and **Schemas**) so it has **construct validity** (it fits into the wider construct of memory theory).

It has also been tested by many researchers besides **Geiselman & Fisher** – as shown by **Köhnken**'s meta-analysis that reviewed 42 studies less than a decade after the invention of CI. This means it has **concurrent validity** (it is backed up by many studies).

The PEACE MODEL was put forward based on much of the same research and shares CI's focus on *rapport*, different styles of questioning and getting interviewees to offer the truth as they see it rather than passively answering questions. So this too has **construct validity**. **Gudjonsson**'s research into FALSE CONFESSIONS also supports the PEACE MODEL, since it offers another reason to prefer ethical interviewing to standard interviewing besides simple fairness and human rights.

Research into the MISINFORMATION EFFECT (e.g. **Loftus & Palmer, 1974**, p87) shows another benefit of CI since it trains interviewers to avoid LEADING QUESTIONS.

Weaknesses

CI generates more information from witnesses than standard interviewing, but this includes more false information too, according to **Köhnken *et al.* (1999)**. The sheer amount of information generated by CI and ethical interviewing can become a problem, since it is time-consuming to sift through it for what is relevant.

Not all witnesses respond well to CI. **Geiselmann (1999)** found that with children under-6, accuracy of recall went *down* using CI, probably because of the complexity of the instructions.

CI can cause ETHICAL problems by asking a witness or victim to go over and over traumatic experiences. This is particularly a problem with investigating rape or interviewing survivors of terror attacks.

Differences

CI and PEACE both focus on establishing *RAPPORT* (a close intimate relationship) and EMPATHY (being sensitive to the interviewee's feelings). However, they do this for different reasons.

CI values *rapport* because reducing stress helps witnesses to recall more clearly; empathy helps the interviewer understand what the interviewee is telling them. However, PEACE values *rapport* and empathy because they show more compassion for the suspect and help to respect their dignity and human rights.

Applications

CI is used today in many police forces across the world. It has been developed for use with children and in social work and psychiatry. In fact, the CI used by Fisher with the Miami police was the **enhanced cognitive interview**. The enhanced-CI downplays the use of **different perspectives** and **changing order** in favour of **listening skills** and building *rapport* (empathy and closeness) with the witness.

There are practical problems with both CI and PEACE. For example, serial killers may strike several times and time is of the essence to save lives. Since both CI and PEACE are more time-consuming than standard interviewing, lives may be put at risk by the delay.

There is also the **'Ticking Bomb Dilemma'** where police have only a short amount of time to get very specific information from a suspect (such as the location of a terrorist bomb in a big city). Many people argue that the biggest moral responsibility here it to save lives by discovering the location of the bomb, not to respect the terrorist's dignity and rights.

However, others argue that you are in fact more likely to get a terrorist to reveal a ticking time bomb by establishing *rapport* and empathy rather than using coercion. This links to the GOOD LIVES MODEL of **case formulation**, because it assumes that even terrorists have good life goals that they are pursuing in a mistaken way and are not really *"moral strangers"*.

A real-life example of this dilemma occurred in 2002 in Germany. 11-year-old **Jakob Von Metzler** was kidnapped and held for ransom. The kidnapper was arrested but refused to say where they boy was imprisoned. **Wolfgang Daschner**, the Deputy Chief of Police, threatened to torture the kidnapper, who immediately gave up the information. However, when police arrived at the site, the boy was already dead.

Because German law forbids the coercion of witnesses under any circumstances, the Deputy was himself arrested and fined (a light sentence: the normal punishment would be 5 years in prison).

FURTHER REFLECTIONS

Police forces have been slow to take up many of the techniques suggested by psychologists (such as **sequential identity line-ups** and CI). This is because police officers tend to prefer traditional methods and *"what works"* rather than new innovations. Techniques like PEACE have been enforced by the Government; CI is slowly becoming more common in police investigations.

However, graduates are increasingly 'fast tracked' in the UK police forces and the **College of Policing** wants all police recruits to have degrees by 2020. This will change the culture of policing and perhaps lead to the wider use of psychological techniques.

JURY DECISION-MAKING

In British law, criminal innocence or guilt is decided by a JURY, which is a panel of 12 members of the public (aged 18-75) who have been randomly selected. The jury follows an entire court case, meets to discuss the evidence and then presents a VERDICT: guilty, innocent or (in Scotland) not proven.

> *In fact, less than 1% of cases are tried by juries, but these are usually the most serious crimes with the most severe sentences.*

A person who sits in a jury is a JUROR. The person being accused of a crime is the DEFENDENDANT. Jurors do not get to speak to the defendant. Instead, they listen to lawyers for the PROSECUTION and DEFENSE who will cross-examine the defendant and other witnesses.

Sometimes a judge might request an EXPERT WITNESS to address the jury about a specialist aspect of the case (such as **Elizabeth Loftus** addressing US juries on the subject of false memories).

One of the jurors is elected to be a FOREMAN (or FOREWOMAN) who will report back to the judge. This person can have a lot of influence on the final verdict. The jury then retires to a quiet room to DELIBERATE (discuss the verdict). Often, the judge will ask them to come to a UNANIMOUS VERDICT (one they all agree with). If the jurors can't agree, the judge might tell the jury to reach a MAJORITY VERDICT instead (such as 10-2).

If the jury cannot reach a verdict, this is a HUNG JURY (and a hung trial). There may be a re-trial later with a new jury.

Juries are supposed to deliberate without contacting the outside world. When outsiders try to influence a juror to vote one way or another (perhaps with threats or bribes), this is JURY TAMPERING. There is a growing problem with jurors using smartphones to use the Internet to research the crime or contact witnesses or defendants. This is not allowed: the jury is supposed to reach a verdict based *purely* on the evidence presented in court. Jurors have been sent to prison for misusing the Internet in this way.

After the trial, jurors are not allowed to discuss the deliberations with *anyone*, not even close friends and relatives. This is the CONFIDENTIALITY OF JURY DELIBERATIONS. It is supposed to protect jurors from being blamed for the verdict and prevent verdicts being challenged. However, it also makes it difficult to conduct psychological research on how juries behave and how they reach their decisions.

Criminological psychologists have developed methods for investigating juries:

- **MOCK JURY:** A group of 12 people form a jury and deliberate on an unreal case. The mock jury might involve a courtroom, with actors playing the judge, lawyers, defendant and witnesses. More often, the mock jury is just given a package of information about the case to read then discuss. Often, the case will be a real one from the past (and the mock jurors won't be told the real verdict that was reached).
- **SHADOW JURY:** A group of people form a jury and follow a real case as it is happening (usually from the **public gallery** in a courtroom). Law firms sometimes employ shadow juries for cases to help them understand how best to prosecute or defend cases. Sometimes, the shadow jury deliberates and reaches their own verdict (which might not be the same as the real jury); sometimes they are just interviewed or surveyed about their impressions.

Deciding guilt or innocence is what psychologists call an ATTRIBUTION. A psychological process affecting attributions is the JUST WORLD HYPOTHESIS (JWH). This is a deeply-held belief (a SCHEMA) that the world is a fair place where good things happen to good people and bad things only happen to bad people. Since most of us view ourselves as 'good people' the JWH is very important for our emotional wellbeing (we need to believe bad things aren't going to happen to us).

In juries, JWH can lead to a phenomenon called BLAMING THE VICTIM. This when we assume that, because something bad happened to this person, this must be a bad person: they 'got what they deserved'. This is sometimes seen in sexual crimes where attractive female victims are seen as provoking the attack (e.g. by their dress).

CHARACTERISTICS OF THE DEFENDANT

Appearance

The HALO EFFECT (**Karen Dion, 1972**) is a well-known process where observers ATTRIBUTE positive characteristics (like honesty) to people they find attractive. This sort of irrational thinking is known in Psychology as an ATTRIBUTION ERROR. This is why lawyers advise defendants to dress well and look as presentable as possible in court.

Taylor & Butcher (2007) asked 96 volunteers (half White, half Black) to read a transcript of a fictional mugging case. Participants were shown a photograph of either an attractive or unattractive defendant, asked to rate guilt on a 0-5 scale and suggest a length of sentence. Unattractive defendants were almost 50% more likely to be found guilty (mean 4.4 compared to 2.3) and got longer sentences (7 months compared to 4). However, the race of the defendant did not make a significant difference (*c.f.* p53).

Wilbur Castello et al. (1990) tested 145 **mock jurors** (71 males, 74 females) who read a summary of a case in which a 23-yr old secretary accused her male employer of sexual harassment (making sexual remarks and attempting to kiss and fondle her). Mock jurors were shown one of two photographs of the defendant (the boss) and the plaintiff (secretary) and asked to decide whether or not the defendant was guilty:

Plaintiff is	Guilty verdict when Defendant is	
	Attractive	Unattractive
Attractive	71%	83%
Unattractive	41%	69%

This suggests that juries make decisions based on STEREOTYPES and SCHEMAS that criminals are unattractive people (and perhaps based on **Lombroso**'s old theory about criminal types).

McKelvie & Coley (1993) asked mock jurors to judge the guilt of attractive and unattractive defendants for robbery and for robbery leading to murder. Attractive robbers were less likely to be convicted but this effect disappeared for murderers, suggesting jurors can set aside their bias in serious cases.

Gender

Men are four times more represented in the Criminal Justice System (CJS) than women – and women are barely represented at all for the most serious crimes of violence. This leads to strong stereotypes (SCHEMAS) that women do not commit such crimes. Some argue for the CHIVALRY HYPOTHESIS, which is that juries and judges are lenient on women, viewing them as unlucky rather than criminal.

McCoy & Gray (2007) conclude that **mock jurors** view female defendants as more believable than male defendants in a fictional case of child sexual abuse.

Thompson et al. (2011) gave 24 **mock jurors** a case to consider where the defendant was either male or female, high social class or low social class and either showed emotion in the courtroom or remained unemotional. There was no significant difference in guilty verdicts but mock jurors judged female defendants more leniently when choosing between them being guilty of murder (serious) or guilty of manslaughter (less serious):

Defendant is:	Mock Jury found defendant guilty of:	
	Murder	Manslaughter
Male	23%	26%
Female	20%	28%

The opposite view is DOUBLE-JEOPARDY. This is the idea that juries punish women more harshly than men because they not only break the law but also go against our schemas of feminine behaviour. In effect they are punished twice: for their crime and for being 'unfeminine'.

Wayne *et al.* (2001) found that, in considering a case of workplace sexual harassment, mock jurors were more likely to find a woman guilty of harassing a man than a man of harassing a woman (but same-gender harassers were viewed most negatively of all).

In the above study by **Thompson *et al.* (2011)**, mock jurors recommended longer sentences to female defendants who did not show emotion, especially if they were low social class:

> *Male defendants from a high socio-economic status, and who appear to be upset or distressed by the situation receive a harsher sentence, and females who are from a low socio-economic status and show no emotional effect by the situation receive a harsher sentence* – **Simon Thompson**

Ethnicity

There's a widespread belief that juries evaluate defendants based on the colour of their skin, being more likely to find black & minority ethnicity (BME) defendants guilty of more serious crimes with harsher sentences.

26% of UK prisoners are from BME backgrounds, but only 13% of the wider UK population are BME (source: **Prison Reform Trust, 2018**). In the USA, 1 in every 15 black men is in prison, compared to 1:36 Latinos and 1:106 white males (source: **American Civil Liberties Union**).

Allport & Postman (1947) showed participants a drawing (*below*) of an argument on a subway train: the black character is well dressed; the white character is scruffy and holds a knife.

Participants had to describe the scene to another participant who described it to another; this is SERIAL REPRODUCTION (like the game of *Chinese Whispers*).

After several stages of serial reproduction, white participants tended to reverse the appearances of the characters, describing a respectable white man and a scruffy black character; some even described the black character *holding the knife*. This seems to be due to racist SCHEMAS affecting how people remember events and attribute blame.

In a similar study, **Birt Duncan (1976)** asked white American students to watch a filmed conversation between a black and a white co-worker arguing about pensions. When the white person gently shoved the black person, this was interpreted as violent by only 13% of the participants; when the black person did the shoving, 73% interpreted it as violent.

However, although these studies show racists SCHEMAS in action, they are not jury studies. Juries are carefully instructed only to find someone guilty if it is *"beyond all reasonable doubt"* and are told to set any prejudices aside.

Pfeifer & Ogloff (1991) formed a **mock jury** of white university students who read a description of a rape case with either a white defendant or a black defendant. The black defendant was rates as more guilty than the white defendant. However, this effect vanished when the mock jurors were instructed beforehand to avoid prejudice.

Cheryl Thomas (*Are Juries Fair?* 2010) put these ideas to the test with a highly realistic procedure. Thomas used SIMULATED TRIALS. These were fictional filmed trials based on real cases, with real judges, lawyers and police as the actors, shot in real courts. The all-white mock jurors used were real juries (although assembled to sit on different cases: they watched these simulated trials after finishing their real jury service). Juries were from Nottingham (an ethnically diverse city) and Winchester (a rural town).

The case was a man accused of Actual Bodily Harm (ABM) after a fight outside a bar. The defendant was White, Black or Asian in different versions. The original case resulted in a hung jury.

Verdict:	20 Juries in Nottingham		21 Juries in Winchester	
	White Defendant	**BME Defendant**	**White Defendant**	**BME Defendant**
Guilty	2	0	1	1
Not Guilty	5	4	3	4
Hung Jury	3	6	6	6

The juries tended to agree with the original hung jury, with very little difference based on the ethnicity of the defendant (with Nottingham juries slightly more likely to find a white defendant to be guilty).

Cheryl Thomas concludes there is no evidence for the race of the defendant affecting jury decision-making.

PRE-TRIAL PUBLICITY

PRE-TRIAL PUBLICITY (PTP) is when *jurors hear about the case through news media before the trial starts*. This means they may already have an impression of the defendant's innocence or guilt. In particular, news reports might reveal the background of the defendant or the victim (such as previous criminal convictions) which would *not* be revealed to a jury in court (because the jury is being asked to find the defendant innocent or guilty of this particular crime based on the evidence, not on anyone's past record).

In the UK, as soon as a suspect is arrested, reporters will be in CONTEMPT OF COURT if they reveal more details about the case. This is why news commentators often use the expression: *"A man [or woman] is helping police with their enquiries."* Reporters are also banned from interviewing witnesses before the trial.

If PTP makes it impossible for a jury to be unbiased, the trial may be 'quashed'. For example, in 1997 the trial of 6 prisoners who escaped Whitemoor Prison collapsed after the *London Evening Standard* revealed that 5 had been IRA terrorists. The newspaper was fined £40,000 and there was no re-trial.

However, the rise of online social media has made it hard to enforce these restrictions. In 2016, in a trial of two teenage girls for the murder of Angela Wrightson, the judge had to discharge the jury and order a re-trial in another location because people were publishing hostile information about the defendants on *FaceBook*.

Jurors are instructed not to use smartphones and laptops to access social media while deliberating. There have been a number of prosecutions of jurors who have done this: in 2013, juror Joseph Beard was jailed for 2 months for using *Google* to research a fraud trial; he was discharged from the jury and a re-trial was ordered.

> *NB. Strictly speaking, looking at news reports **during** the trial is not PRE-trial publicity, so be careful about how you use these examples in the Exam.*

Cheryl Thomas (*Are Juries Fair?* 2010, c.f. p54) looked at the FADE FACTOR: media reports are less likely to affect jurors as time passes and the details 'fade' from memory. Thomas researched 62 cases involving 668 jurors in Nottingham, Winchester and London. Most jurors recalled media reports while the trial was going on, but nothing from before their jury service began.

She found that about a third (35%) of jurors recalled PTP and those in high-profile cases were 70% likely to recall information from PTP compared to 11% in low-profile cases. Around two-thirds of jurors in all the cases could not recall if PTP had emphasised the innocence or guilt of the defendant. The minority who *did* recall the emphasis of PTP tended to think it had implied the defendant was guilty.

Type of case:	Emphasis of PTP on defendant			
	Guilty	Innocent	Neither	Don't remember
High profile	33%	4%	43%	20%
Low profile	30%	2%	53%	15%

20% of jurors who said they remembered PTP found it hard to put the reports out of their mind. This suggests PTP can influence jurors, but only in a minority of high-profile cases and, because of the FADE FACTOR, a re-trial should reduce this problem.

However, **Ruva & McEvoy (2008)** carried out an experiment with a **mock jury** of 320 students who read news articles with PTP, with a third emphasising the defendant's guilt, a third emphasising innocence and a third neutral (the CONTROLS). A week later they watched a video of the trial. Half offered their verdict immediately and half waited for 2 days. There was no difference in the verdicts between the two groups, suggesting the FADE FACTOR did not occur. However, the group exposed to negative PTP had twice as many guilty verdicts as the Control Group with neutral PTP.

The mock jurors were given a memory test which showed they mis-remembered the negative information from PTP as being evidence that had been given in trial. This is an example of CRYPTOMNESIA: the mock jurors forgot that they had received the negative evidence from PTP and believed it had come from the trial itself.

EVALUATION OF PRE-TRIAL PUBLICITY AO3

Credibility

Mock juries become a lot more credible when the samples are not just students, the jurors are advised to be unbiased and the case material is filmed rather than just being a set of handouts. **Ruva & McEvoy (2008)** use a filmed trial and **Pfeifer & Ogloff (1991)** tested the effect of advising jurors to be unbiased. However, **Thomas (2010)** surpasses all the others. Since she had the collaboration of the UK Government, Cheryl Thomas was able to interview *real* jurors and use actual court locations and staff in her simulated trials. This level of **ecological validity** is superior to all the other studies.

MOCK JURIES are a valid technique for testing the precise variables that affect jury decision-making, since different mock-jurors can be exposed to different information about the case to see how this influences their judgement. This is important because the law forbids studying real juries during their deliberations surveying them about their decisions afterwards.

Weaknesses

With the exception of **Thomas (2010)**, all the studies here use mock juries made up of university students, taking part for course credits or cash payment. This introduces the risk of **demand characteristics**, since students will want to 'do the right thing' if they are being rewarded. These mock juries are not representative of the makeup of real juries, which include working people and retired people up to the age of 75. Since most students don't own houses or have children, their attitudes to certain crimes (burglary, crimes against children) might be different from homeowners and parents.

All mock juries (even the ones in **Cheryl Thomas' study**) suffer from the problem that they are not really convicting anybody. No one goes to prison (with all the grief and loss that means for families and loved ones) or walks free (with the possible danger to the public that poses). There are no consequences, so jurors' the choices aren't serious.

Differences

The big contrast is between general studies into memory and attribution bias (e.g. **Allport & Postman**'s study of racist schemas or **Karen Dion**'s study of the Halo Effect), which lead us to expect juries to be very biased, compared to actual jury studies which often reveal no bias at all or only small biases, sometimes in unexpected directions (like **Cheryl Thomas**' all-white Nottingham juries finding the *white* defendant guilty).

One explanation is that people have strong SOCIAL SCRIPTS about how juries should behave (acquired from watching many courtroom dramas on TV and in films) and they consciously set aside their biases in these situations. Thomas' Nottingham juries seem to be an example of the SELF-DEFEATING PROPHECY in action: white jurors are aware of the stereotype of racism and are determined to behave in the opposite way.

Applications

The obvious application is to alter court practices to bring about fairer trials. If juries are biased because of appearance, then witnesses and defendants can give evidence from behind screens; if gender and race influence a jury, then quotas can be used to make sure there is a balanced mix of genders and ethnic groups in a jury. Trial by jury could be abandoned all together if research shows PTP makes it impossible for juries to reach an unbiased verdict.

Lawyers will also make use of this research to win cases. Most lawyers already advise their clients and witnesses to make themselves as attractive as possible when they go into court; perhaps this should extend to full 'makeovers'? In the UK, the prosecution is entitled to ask some jurors to 'stand down' before the trial starts, but this right is rarely used; perhaps it should be used more often for jurors exposed to PTP and perhaps the law should be changed to give the defence this right too?

REVISING EYEWITNESSES, INTERVIEWS & JURIES

DEFINITIONS
BME
CHIVALRY HYPOTHESIS
CONTEXT REINSTATEMENT
CRYPTOMNESIA
EOG
EYEWITNESS TESTIMONY
FACIAL COMPOSITES
FOCUSED RETRIEVAL
HALO EFFECT
MISINFORMATION EFFECT
MOCK JURY
PEACE MODEL
PTP
SCHEMA
WEAPON FOCUS EFFECT

RESEARCH SUMMARIES
ALLPORT & POSTMAN (1947)
CASTELLOW *ET AL.* (1990)
FISHER *ET AL.* (1989)
GABBERT *ET AL.* (2003)
LOFTUS, LOFTUS & MESSO (1987)
LOFTUS & PICKRELL (1995)
PICKEL. (1999)
PFEIFFER & OGLOFF (1991)
RUVA & MCEVOY (2008)
THOMAS (2010)
THOMPSON *ET AL.* (2011)
WELLS *ET AL.* (1998)

RESEARCH
Read one of these articles from the Guardian website
(www.theguardian.com)
Add details to your notes
- 'Some days I think I was molested, others I'm not so sure' (Watt, 2017)
- Helping child witnesses (Williams, 2018)
- Is the Internet destroying juries? (Hirsch, 2010)

COMPREHENSION QUESTIONS
1. What are the problems with police line-ups?
2. What happened to Donald M. Thompson?
3. What does the 'Lost in the Mall' study reveal about post-event information?
4. What are the problems with police interviews?
5. How does a Cognitive Interview work?
6. In what ways are police interviews sometimes unethical?
7. Why do suspects make false confessions?
8. Why is it forbidden to question jurors about their decisions?
9. What are the weaknesses of mock juries?
10. Why is **Thomas (2010)** an important and unusual study of jury decision-making?

EXAM-STYLE QUESTIONS

Lucy has been called to take part in a jury for a case of armed robbery. She thinks she remembers a news story about the crime, which described the man who robbed the bank as a 'psycho'. Lucy is worried that she might not be able to have an unbiased view of the defendant.

(a) Describe what is meant by pre-trial publicity. [2 marks AO1]

(b) Explain one strength and one weakness of eyewitness testimony in court. [4 marks AO3]

(c) Using your knowledge of Psychology, explain and evaluate whether a juror like Lucy can reach an unbiased decision. [16 marks AO1+AO2+AO3]

CRIMINOLOGICAL PSYCHOLOGY: METHODS

What's this topic about?

This introduces you to the main methodologies in Child Psychology, in particular the use of EXPERIMENTS and CASE STUDIES. You will also look again at **eyewitness testimony** research from a methods angle, consider data analysis and revisit ethics with a focus on the importance of the HCPC for forensic psychologists.

You will have covered some of these ideas already as part of the AS or Year 1 course and in **Unit 2A (Clinical Psychology)**:

Experiments

Experiments were introduced as part of the **Cognitive Approach**: **Baddeley** used a LAB EXPERIMENT to test memory recall that used INDEPENDENT GROUPS (comparing different lists of words) and REPEATED MEASURES (testing the same people on the same words over and over to see how they improved). In the **Biological Approach**, **Raine et al.** used a NATURAL EXPERIMENT to compare NGRI murderers with non-criminals (this was a natural experiment because Raine had no control over who was in each group; it was a naturally-occurring variable). In the **Learning Approach**, **Bandura**'s 'Bobo Doll' studies were both LAB EXPERIMENTS (testing imitation of different types of role models) and NATURAL EXPERIMENTS (comparing girls and boys). In the **Social Approach**, **Sherif**'s 'Robbers Cave' study is a FIELD EXPERIMENT which tests real schoolboys in a real summer camp.

Case Studies

Case Studies were introduced in the **Cognitive Approach** with the case of H.M. whose brain damaged prevented him from making new memories. You also explored case studies as part of **Clinical Psychology** (the Specification recommends **Lavarenne et al.** but **psychologywizard.net** recommends **Bradshaw**'s case study of Carol being treated for schizophrenia with CBT).

Eyewitness Testimony

EWT was introduced as part of the **Cognitive Approach** and could be used as the basis for the Cognitive Key Question or Cognitive Practical. The MULTI-STORE MODEL explains how eyewitnesses can fail to **attend** to details or fail to **rehearse** them afterwards and how memory traces can **decay** or be **displaced** by competing information. **Bartlett**'s idea of SCHEMAS ties into to **Tulving**'s theory that LONG TERM MEMORY is encodes SEMANTICALLY and we recall things based on what they *mean* to us.

Health & Care Practitioners Council (HCPC)

The HCPC was introduced as part of **Clinical Psychology**. It is an organisation that regulates practitioner psychologists (including forensic psychologists), holding them to its 15 STANDARDS OF PROFICIENCY (such as CONFIDENTIALITY, NON-DISCRIMINATION and PROFESSIONAL BOUNDARIES).

EXPERIMENTS

Experiments were introduced in **Unit 1** so this section revises the main points about experiments then provides applications for Criminological Psychology.

Experiment is...	Meaning	Advantage	Disadvantage
Laboratory	The experimenter manipulates the IV and measures the DV in a controlled environment	Reveals CAUSE-AND-EFFECT: IV causes changes in DV	Often highly artificial; not GENERALISABLE to real life; prone to DEMAND CHARACTERISTICS
Field	The experimenter manipulates the IV and measures the DV in a real-world environment	Less artificial, more generalisable to real life; less demand characteristics	Many CONFOUNDING VARIABLES prevent clear proof of cause-and-effect
Natural/Quasi	The experimenter observes the effects of a naturally-occurring IV (can be lab or field)	Enables study of IVs that would be impossible or unethical to manipulate	Does not show cause-and-effect as participants not randomly assigned to conditions of the IV
Independent Groups	Each participant experiences just one condition of the experiment's IV	No ORDER EFFECTS (and therefore less demand characteristics)	PARTICIPANT VARIABLES as people in each condition not identical
Repeated Measures	Each participant experiences every condition of the experiment's IV	Removes participant variables as same people in each condition	Order effects lead to improvement or fatigue and increase demand characteristics
Matched Pairs	Each participant experiences just one condition of the IV but is matched against a participant in another condition	No order effects as test not repeated but also reduced participant variables as participants very similar	Participant variables still present as participants not identical; inconvenient to set up; matching people on variables may lead to more demand characteristics

The main strength of all experiments is that you are OPERATIONALISING the main variables to create EMPIRICAL EVIDENCE (it's based on the 5 senses). This sort of evidence can be shared with other people. This is important for the SCIENTIFIC STATUS of psychological research.

Another strength is that experiments reveal CAUSALITY – they show CAUSE-AND-EFFECT at work and this is important for turning a HYPOTHESIS into a scientific theory. Lab experiments are the most powerful method for exploring cause-and-effect because all the other variables can be CONTROLLED, so if the DV changes it must be the IV causing it.

The main weakness of experiments is that some variables are difficult to OPERATIONALISE or CONTROL. Criminality is a difficult variable to operationalise (do you focus on actual convictions or include fantasies and urges?) and it's hard to control for factors like drug use, poor education, peer pressure and unhappy childhoods.

Another weakness is that experiments can be low in ECOLOGICAL VALIDITY if they are artificial. This is important because, in unrealistic situations, participants behave unnaturally and are not REPRESENTATIVE of how they would act outside of the experiment. For example, brain scans, memory test and mock juries are all unusual situations that don't resemble the situations of actual criminals, eyewitnesses and jurors.

EXPERIMENTS USED IN CRIMINOLOGICAL PSYCHOLOGY

Studies that compare PSYCHOPATHS to ordinary people (such as **Yang et al.** or **Blair et al.**) are natural experiments with independent groups design. Research comparing males and females is always a natural experiment.

Studies into LABELLING (such as **Rosenthal & Jacobson**) are usually lab or field experiments, although **Madon et al.** (p17) was a natural experiment as it looked at mothers who had already labelled their children. If they compare the children before and after labelling (such as Rosenthal & Jacobson), this is repeated measures design. If they compare participants who have been labelled with those who haven't (such as Madon et al.), this is independent groups design. **Raine et al. (1997)** matched NGRI murders to controls on things like schizophrenia. However, it wasn't a matched pairs design because all Raine did was make sure there were 6 schizophrenics in each group – he didn't specifically compare each schizophrenic with a schizophrenic in the other condition.

Research into EWT or MOCK JURIES is usually a **lab experiment**, randomly assigning participants to a **control group** who get a normal recall task or case to study and an **experimental group** whose recall is interfered with or whose exposure to the case is different in some way (e.g. the way **Cheryl Thomas** varies the ethnicity of the defendant or **Castellow et al.** changes the attractiveness of the defendant and plaintiff).

Research into the effects of TREATMENT PROGRAMMES are usually **field experiments** (comparing offenders getting the treatment with others who don't, or who get a PLACEBO as with **Gesh et al.** and **Zaalberg et al.**). A rare field experiment using real eyewitnesses to a real crime was **Yuille & Cutshall (1986, p70)**. **Geiselman & Fisher** tested the COGNITIVE INTERVIEW in a **field experiment**, randomly assigning real Miami police officers to CI-training or standard interviewing.

EVALUATING EXPERIMENTS IN CRIMINOLOGICAL PSYCHOLOGY AO3

Natural experiments (such as psychopath studies, investigations into the warrior-gene or gender comparisons) suffer from a major problem: the participants have not been randomly assigned to each condition. This means that the psychopaths or the MAOA-carriers or men might be different from the people they are being compared with in lots of ways. In a TRUE EXPERIMENT, the participants are all the same (or as similar as possible) except for the IV. You can never know this in a natural experiment.

> *Perhaps psychopaths all have something else in common, like abusive upbringings or head injuries – and **that** is what is really causing their behaviour. Think about all the ways that women have different experiences from men and you'll see why comparing them with each other isn't at all straightforward.*

On the other hand, the **true lab experiments** such as EWT or mock juries are usually deeply unrealistic and they almost always have to be independent groups design because you never know when a crime is going to happen, so you can't study eyewitnesses before and after. There are legal restrictions on researching real jurors in real trials.

However, there are exceptions. **Thomas' 2010 research** (*Are Jurors Fair?*) used real jurors and created a mock trial that was very realistic. **Yuille & Cutshall (1986**, p70**)** were lucky to be able to test actual eyewitnesses to a street shooting shortly after the crime had happened. But even these aren't perfect: Thomas still used a mock trial, not a real one, and Yuille & Cutsall could only test the eyewitnesses once the police had finished with them (and the main eyewitness, the shopowner who was shot, didn't take part.

The main **field experiments** are studies like **Gesh *et al.*** who gave half the prisoners a diet supplement and the others a placebo. These were real prisoners in a real prison, so it was high in ecological validity. **Geiselman & Fisher** were also unusual in being able to test real police carrying out real interviews. However, the realism itself causes problems because the researchers couldn't control all the confounding variables going on:

- Did the prisoners detect the real omega-3 pills by their smell? Did they swap pills or not even swallow them at all (like the psychiatric patients in **Rosenhan**'s study)
- Were other changes happening at the prison (such as changes in staff, crackdowns on drugs or the arrival of new prisoners)?
- Were other changes happening at the Miami police precinct (such as new recruits, changes in the local gangs' behaviours, pay rises or officers retiring) which affected the interviews?

> *Most of the studies into genes and upbringing, such as the **Cambridge Study in Delinquent Development (CSDD)**, aren't experiments at all: they are CORRELATIONS which, as everyone knows, don't show causation.*

CASE STUDIES

Case Studies were introduced in Unit 1 so this section revises the main points then provides applications for Criminological Psychology. A case study is *an in-depth study of a single person or a small group that all share a single characteristic* (like a family).

Case studies are usually **longitudinal studies** – they take place over a period of time, typically months. Case studies usually use a mixture of methods. Older case studies (like those by **Freud**) used to focus on **interviews** and **observations** and collect **qualitative data**. More recent case studies mix this qualitative approach with **questionnaires** and **biological measures** (like brain scans or genetic profiling) to collect **quantitative data**.

Case Study is...	Meaning	Advantage	Disadvantage
Retrospective	Focus on historical information	Identify risk factors and explanations	Not all the historical information may be available or reliable
Prospective	Longitudinal, following participant cover a period of time	Reveals how behaviour changes	HAWTHORNE EFFECT – participant may be influenced by the study
Instrumental	Determine effectiveness of a measure or treatment	Show that a procedure (e.g. offender treatment) works	Not an experiment so does not prove cause-and-effect
Ideographic	Descriptive and qualitative research	Rich data, in-depth understanding	Doesn't test hypotheses or demonstrate scientific laws in action
Nomothetic	Predictive and quantitative research	Tests hypotheses and reveals scientific laws in action	Lacks rich, in-depth data
Quantitative	Data is in the form of numbers or tallies	Suitable for statistical analysis, reliable, objective	Reductionist, may lack insight into real thoughts
Qualitative	Data is in the form of words	Rich detail, may produce insight into real thoughts	Not suitable for statistical analysis, unreliable, subjective

The main strength of all case studies is that you are focusing on an individual (or small group) in detail, gaining the sort of understanding that could never be acquired through simple surveys, observations or experiments.

Another strength is that case studies explore unusual cases and exceptional situations; they focus on the sort of ANOMALIES or OUTLIERS that are usually discounted from **nomothetic research** because they would 'skew' the data.

A weakness of case studies is that they cannot **generalise** their findings from single individuals (especially unusual ones) to the population at large.

Another weakness is that case studies are often SUBJECTIVE: they are strongly base on the researcher's personal view of the participant(s). Due to the close study going on, researchers often form working relationships with the participants in case studies and view them as people, not just as 'subjects' or 'cases'. The participants often get to know the researchers too.

CASE STUDIES USED IN CHILD PSYCHOLOGY

Freud (1909) used case studies with his patients, notably his case study of 5-year-old 'Little Hans' who suffered behavioural problems (a crippling phobia of horses) which Freud believed was caused by the boy's unconscious hatred of his father.

Brunner *et al.* (1996, p9**)** carried out a case study of a Dutch family which carried a gene that gave the males a strong predisposition towards antisocial behaviour, including criminality. The study lasted 15 years and was largely RETROSPECTIVE (analysing 5 generations of men in the family and going back through the family tree). The study was also INSTRUMENTAL, since it tested the hypothesis that a mutant MONOAMINE OXIDASE-A (MAOA) gene on the X-chromosome was passed on within the family and present in the men who offended.

Whitehead *et al.* (2007, p31, 33**)** carried out a case study on a Maori gangster from New Zealand identified as '**Mr C.**' The study focused on **case formulation** and **offender treatment**. It was RETROSPECTIVE (examining Mr C's childhood and criminal past), PROJECTIVE (following Mr C through his treatment programme and experiences once released) and INSTRUMENTAL (testing the value of the GOOD LIVES MODEL of treatment).

EVALUATING CASE STUDIES IN CRIMINOLOGICAL PSYCHOLOGY AO3

Whitehead's case study of **Mr C** is a good example of the detailed and intimate nature of IDEOGRAPHIC case studies. Mr C opened up about his past, his goals and his inner conflicts, particularly between his own desire for a 'good life' and his loyalty to his gang. As an uneducated man, he could not express himself clearly so a Maori counsellor who shared his culture was employed to be his mentor.

The study traces Mr C abandoning his violent and abusive language, forming goals like going to university, wrestling with relapses into drug-use and violence and the delight of his family when he starts his university course (which involves a pledge to the Dean not to bring drugs or gang-members onto the campus).

As a Maori gangster, Mr C might be discounted from many studies of offenders as too unusual. However, he might also be too unusual for his experiences to be **generalised** to other prisoners going through an offender treatment programme.

> *the specific cultural interventions may not generalizable to European New Zealanders and prisoners in other parts of the world* – **Paul Whitehead**

However, Whitehead argues that the case study might be generalisable to treating offenders from 'indigenous cultures' who are underrepresented in standard criminological psychology. Instrumentally, it shows the effectiveness of the GOOD LIVES MODEL (p33) because it focuses on culture.

Brunner's case study of the Dutch family with the mutant MAOA gene is the opposite sort of research. It studies a family, not an individual, and is strongly NOMOTHETIC, focusing on scientifically testable genetic links rather than personal testimony. This means it does not suffer from the problem of SUBJECTIVITY in other case studies.

The family's genetic disorder is very rare, making them anomalies in normal research and unrepresentative of normal criminals. However, the conclusions do tell us that genes can be responsible for aggressive behaviour in at least *some* offenders and if the Dutch men from this family behaved in extremely antisocial ways because of completely defective MAOA genes, other offenders might commit crimes because they have partially-defective MAOA genes.

The Finnish study by **Tilhonen *et al.* (2015**, p9**)** supports the link between MAOA and offending. **Xandra Breakefield (1993)** proposes that if offending is linked to a genetic disorder, it could be corrected with diet or drugs that regulate the body's production of neurotransmitters.

SAMPLING

Sampling introduced in **Unit 1** so this section revises the main points then provides applications for Criminological Psychology.

Sample is...	Meaning	Advantage	Disadvantage
Opportunity	Choosing participants who are convenient (available at the time)	Easy, quick, inexpensive	Experimenter bias by choosing unrepresentative participants
Random	Choosing participants in an unbiased way (e.g. names from a hat)	No bias	Requires list of all possible participants; random selection can still be unrepresentative
Self-selecting (volunteer)	Advertising then choosing any participants who respond	No experimenter bias	Time consuming, participant bias as people who respond may be unrepresentative
Stratified	Opportunity or volunteer sample including numbers of people in different categories (strata)	Will be representative of the strata used	Time consuming, choice of strata may be biased (e.g. researcher might miss out important strata like race)

Samples are representative if they contain the same mix of people that are found in the TARGET POPULATION. Samples tend to be unrepresentative if the selection was BIASED (the research didn't include important people for personal reasons) or if it contains too many ANOMALIES (unusual people who will SKEW the results).

- Making a sample larger does NOT make it more representative
- However, large samples may contain fewer ANOMALIES who would skew the results of a small sample

The best way to make a sample representative is to STRATIFY it (making sure you contain the same proportion of men, women, different ethnicities, rich and poor, ages, etc. that are found in the target population). However, it's not always obvious which strata are important and which are not. For example, many early Psychology studies (like **Milgram**) didn't include women or (like **Sherif**) ethnic minorities.

> *Do you think star sign (e.g. Gemini, Virgo and Scorpio) is an important strata? Should Criminological Psychology studies make sure that 1/12th of the sample is from each sign of the Zodiac? Most Psychologists don't think so – but maybe they're wrong!*

If you sample this tasty sauce, you might get a bit with a chilli in it and think it's hotter than it really is. That would be an anomaly skewing your data. If you take a really BIG sample, a single chilli won't spoil it

SAMPLING USED IN CRIMINOLOGICAL PSYCHOLOGY

Most of the studies into EYEWITNESS TESTIMONY or JURY DECISION-MAKING use samples of university students. These are usually recruited through **volunteer sampling** and rewarded with cash or (in America) college credits.

Studies into criminality often use prisoners. For example, **Jacobs et al. (1965, p10)** looked for XYY abnormalities in 197 Scottish prisoners in psychiatric hospitals while **Tilhonnen et al. (2015, p9)** studied 900 prisoners in Finland. Studies into PSYCHOPATHS, like **Yang et al. (2009), Glenn et al. (2009)** and **Blair et al. (1996)** all used prisoners who had been identified as psychopaths using the HARE PSYCHOPATHY CHECKLIST (PCL). These studies are opportunity samples, since they use criminals who happen to be in the prison system at the time.

A different sample was recruited by **Gesh et al. (2002, p34)** for his research into the link between diet and aggression. **Bernard Gesh** couldn't get prisoners in Aylesbury to agree until he made a personal appeal to the toughest character in the prison: this inmate recruited other prisoners for Gesh, which is a **snowball sample**.

The **Cambridge Study in Delinquent Development (CSDD, p16)** uses a cohort of males who were born in South London in 1953. The boys were taken from the registers of primary schools within a mile of the researchers' office: this is an **opportunity sample**.

Other interesting opportunity samples include **Fisher *et al.* (1989)** who recruited police officers from the Miami Police Department to test the COGNITIVE INTERVIEW and **Thomas (2010)** who recruit members of real jurors in Nottingham, Winchester and London to test JURY DECISION-MAKING.

EVALUATING SAMPLING IN CRIMINOLOGICAL PSYCHOLOGY AO3

The biggest problem with samples in Criminological Psychology is that researchers rarely get to study actual criminals or the witnesses or victims to real crimes.

Criminals do not present themselves to be studied and discuss their offending. Instead, psychologists have to make do with convicted and (usually) imprisoned criminals. Some of these convicted offenders may in fact be innocent. For the rest, the fact that they have been caught and sentenced marks them out as a certain sort of criminal: the unsuccessful sort. The most successful criminals don't get caught and therefore don't get studied.

Another problem with using prisoners is that they have to agree to being in the study. Many prisoners will do this because they think (rightly or wrongly) that it will impress a parole board, making it more likely they will be released early. This is a strong likelihood for DEMAND CHARACTERISTICS, since the prisoners will want to behave in the way that (they think) the researcher wants.

PSYCHOPATHS are a particular problem because they are *"glib"* and *"manipulative"* and will try to get on good terms with researchers in order to turn things to their advantage.

A related problem is that prison-based studies tend to use only prisoners who are intelligent, reasonably well-behaved and not mentally-ill. These prisoners are a minority within the overall prison population, which contains a lot of people with learning disorders, drug problems and mental health problems. This creates extreme versions of the problems of **opportunity sampling**: choosing only a certain sort of (unrepresentative) participant.

Whitehead *et al.* (2007, p31, 33**)** focused on Mr C, who was a violent drug abuser. However, Mr C was already in a COGNITIVE-BEHAVIOURAL TREATMENT PROGRAMME because he had a desire (in a confused sort of way) to turn his life around. This makes Mr C different from the sort of hardened offenders who have no intention of changing.

The **Cambridge Study (CSDD**, p16**)** was a longitudinal study of working class boys up into their 40s. Many did pick up criminal records, so this was a rare opportunity to study criminals in detail before and after their offending.

Since researchers don't know when crimes are going to happen, they can't be on hand to study victims or witnesses straight away. The police don't allow researchers to 'interfere' with cases and it can take years to close a case, by which point memories have faded. There are exceptions. **Yuille & Cutshall (1986**, p70**)** got to study the eyewitnesses to a street shooting in Vancouver, Canada because the thief (who had robbed a gun shop) was shot and killed by the owner in self-defence. This unusual case was settled very quickly and there was a large number of witnesses for who the details were still fresh and recent.

The law in most countries forbids research real jurors during a court case and even afterwards.

Psychologists get around these problems by recruiting student volunteers to be **eyewitnesses** or **mock jurors**. This is convenient (since most psychologists work in universities and most students are keen to earn cash or course credits). However, it has problems. Student samples tend to be unrepresentative in age (teens or early twenties), educational level (high) and social class (usually middle-class, from comfortable backgrounds).

The majority of victims of crime and witnesses to crime are likely to be from poorer backgrounds and less educated, so students are not representative of typical eyewitnesses.

Middle class professionals (e.g. teachers, doctors, nurses, dentists, Members of Parliament) can apply to be 'exempted' (let off) from jury duty on the grounds that they can't be spared from their important jobs. This means educated middle class people might not be very representative of typical jurors either.

The problem of 'jury-dodging' by middle class professionals used to be more serious but the Government changed the law in 2004 to make it harder for lawyers, doctors, etc. to get out of jury service.

REVISING EXPERIMENTS, CASE STUDIES & SAMPLES

DEFINITIONS
FIELD EXPERIMENT
INDEPENDENT GROUPS DESIGN
INSTRUMENTAL CASE STUDY
LAB EXPERIMENT
MATCHED PAIRS DESIGN
NATURAL EXPERIMENT
OPPORTUNITY SAMPLE
PROJECTIVE CASE STUDY
QUALITATIVE DATA
QUANTITATIVE DATA
RANDOM SAMPLE
REPEATED MEASURES DESIGN
RETROSPECTIVE CASE STUDY
SEMI-STRUCTURED INTERVIEW
STRATIFIED SAMPLE
VOLUNTEER SAMPLE

PROVIDE RESEARCH EXAMPLES OF:
LAB EXPERIMENT
FIELD EXPERIMENT
OPPORTUNITY SAMPLING
CASE STUDY
RANDOM SAMPLING
VOLUNTEER SAMPLING

COMPREHENSION QUESTIONS
1. Why do experiments reveal cause-and-effect?
2. Give an example of a lab experiment and explain specifically what is unrealistic about it.
3. Give an example of a field experiment and explain specifically what confounding variables might affect it.
4. Provide an example of participant variables interfering with a study with independent groups design.
5. Why was **Raine *et al.*** not *strictly speaking* a study with matched pairs design?
6. Give an example of a case study and its advantages.
7. What is wrong with small sample sizes?
8. How can bias be reduced in sampling?
9. What are the problems with sampling prisoners?
10. What are the problems with sampling students for mock juries?

RESEARCH
Find out more about the study by **Yuille & Cuthall (1986)** that involved real eyewitnesses to a dramatic shooting in broad daylight: *c.f.* pp61, 62, 69, 73, 86, 88, 89, 95
You can find a good handout at **www.smartalevels.co.uk** or a web page summary at **a2edexcelpsychology.weebly.com/yuille-and-cutshall-1986.html**

EXAM-STYLE QUESTIONS

Julio wants to know if eyewitness testimony is influenced by physical attractiveness. He gives two groups of students a news story about a (fictional) criminal, one with a picture of a handsome offender, one with an ordinary-looking offender. He records how many participants pick the correct offender out of a line-up of photographs.

(a) State the meaning of an experiment with independent groups design. [2 marks AO1]

(b) Explain how Julio could investigate the same research question as a repeated measures design. [4 marks AO2]

(c) Explain and evaluate the use of lab experiments in criminological psychology; you must make reference to Julio in your answer. [16 marks AO1+AO2+AO3]

METHODOLOGICAL ISSUES IN RESEARCH

These issues were introduced in **Unit 1** and explored in **Unit 2A (Clinical Psychology)**.

RELIABILITY

Reliability refers to the CONSISTENCY of a study or instrument: *will it produce the same results if carried out again in similar circumstances?*

Reliability is a function of a good procedure in a study and there are several techniques to improve reliability:

- **Standardised procedures** for all researchers to follow
- **Scripted behaviour** for researchers to stick to
- Tried-and-tested **instruments**, like established **questionnaires** and **observational schedules**
- **Scientific instruments**, like **brain imaging techniques**

If a study is reliable, it should also be REPLICABLE: it should be possible for a different researcher to follow the same procedures exactly.

There are ways of assessing the reliability of psychological research:

Reliability is...	Meaning	Advantage	Disadvantage
Inter-rater	Two or more raters (or scorers) go over the data separately	if the study is reliable, they should reach the same findings	Both raters must be trained to the same standard; procedures must be standardised
Test-retest	The test is carried out two or more times and the data is checked (by the same rater)	if the study is reliable, the test should produce the same results every time	Time-consuming (and expensive) to re-run the same tests multiple times
Internal	The test is broken into different components or stages which are carried out separately	if the study is reliable, there should be a **correlation** between the results	Test must be something that *can* be broken into different parts

For example, in a quiz, people who do badly on the first 10 questions should do badly on the last 10 too. If teams do great on some rounds but rubbish on others, the questions aren't all equally difficult and the quiz lacks internal reliability

A lot of early criminology is very unreliable: think of **Lombroso**'s sketch drawings of criminals in prisons and morgues! If someone else had drawn those pictures, they might have looked completely different.

Later research involving **brain imaging techniques** (like the PET SCANS in **Raine**'s study) and **genetic testing** (for example, **Brunner**'s research into the mutant MAOA gene) is much more reliable.

Well-established instruments like the HARE PSYCHPATHY CHECKLIST (PCL) and the EYSENCK PERSONALITY QUESTIONNAIRE (EPQ) are well-established and used in several studies, adding to their reliability (e.g. studies by **Yang**, **Glenn** and **Blair** all identify psychopaths using the PCL).

Modern studies into EYEWITNESS TESTIMONY and JURY DECISION-MAKING use **standardised procedures** and **scripted behaviour** (such as **Thomas**' simulated trial scenes). **Cheryl Thomas**' mock juries were assembled 20 times in each location (Nottingham and Winchester) with similar results, which shows the procedure has **test-retest reliability**.

A criticism of CASE STUDIES is that they are entirely based around one person or group and only carried out once. Often, the procedures change while the study is in progress (for example, during **Brunner**'s study of the Dutch family, new techniques for studying genes became available). These makes such research unreliable.

VALIDITY

Validity refers to the TRUSTWORTHINESS of a study or explanation: *does it measure or explain the things it claims to measure or explain?*

Validity is a function of the study not being interfered with: the absence of CONFOUNDING VARIABLES that could change the results without anyone realising. There are several techniques to improve validity:

- **Experimental method** ensures that the DV is being caused by the IV and nothing else
- **Experimental controls** eliminate confounding variables
- **Naturalistic behaviour** can be produced by using **blind techniques, covert observation** or **deception** of participants
- **Lack of experimenter bias** can be brought about by using **double-blind techniques, randomisation** and **quantitative data**
- **Rich data** can be gathered from willing participants studied in-depth using **qualitative data**

> *You will notice some contradictions here: you can make research more valid by gathering qualitative data on willing participants ... or quantitative data on deceived participants. These are different ways of ensuring you get natural and authentic responses from participants.*

There are ways of assessing the validity of psychological research:

Validity is...	Meaning	Advantage	Disadvantage
Face	Outcome matches ordinary or common-sense expectations (e.g. criminals have troubled childhoods)	Easy to apply by non-psychologists	Subjective
Construct	Outcome fits into a well-established theory (e.g. criminals exposed to antisocial role models)	Easy to research other theories	Invalid if theories are invalid or confounding variables at work
Concurrent	Outcome is the same as found by other tests (e.g. criminals score high for Psychoticism)	Other tests reviewed using META-ANALYSIS	Invalid if other tests are invalid or confounding variables at work
Predictive	If the outcome makes predictions that come true (e.g. people given a negative label will become offenders – and then they do!)	Easy to test predictions with more tests	Time-consuming to carry out more tests
Ecological	Outcome is the same as found in real life situations (e.g. ordinary children imitate TV role models)	Easy to research what happens in real life	Difficult to create realistic research situations

Research focused on the experimental method, controls and lack of bias tends to lack ecological validity even if it possesses the other sorts of validity.

Early criminology tends to have high **face validity** but fails on the other sorts: **Lombroso**'s criminals *look like* what we imagine criminals should look like, but its not based on a good understanding of evolution (lacks **construct validity**) and doesn't predict who will turn out to be an offender (lacks **predictive validity**).

Later research ties together much better – it has **construct** and **concurrent validity**. For example, **Brunner et al. (1996)** found the mutant MAOA gene in the Dutch family of offenders and **Tilhonen et al. (2015)** found that Finnish convicts were 13 times more likely to have defective versions of this gene.

Much research into eyewitnesses link with the well-established theory of SCHEMAS and RECONSTRUCTIVE MEMORY (**construct validity**).

However, they do not always have **concurrent validity**; for example, studies by **Elizabeth Loftus** find eyewitnesses to be unreliable but **Yuille & Cuthall (1986**, p70**)** finds real-life eyewitnesses to be very reliable and unaffected by leading questions.

Similarly, research like **Thomas (2010)** lacks **construct validity** since it goes against what lots of theories (e.g. JUST WORLD THEORY, the HALO EFFECT, SCHEMAS) tell us about how biased decision-making is.

However, it has some **concurrent validity** because it lines up with **Pfeifer & Ogloff (1991)** who found that the biases in mock juries disappeared when they were instructed not to discriminate just like real juries.

CASE STUDIES are often high in validity because they are usually rooted in a theory (**construct validity**) and gather rich data from willing participants (**ecological validity**). For example, **Whitehead *et al.* (2007**, p31, 33**)** studied **Mr C** from a SOCIAL LEARNING THEORY perspective and using the GOOD LIVES MODEL. However, it's difficult to use case studies to make **predictions** about how other people will behave (just because Mr C responded to GLM therapy, it doesn't mean every offender will).

OBJECTIVITY

Objectivity refers to the FACTUAL BASIS of a study or instrument: *will it produce results that do not depend on anyone's personal interpretation?*

Objectivity is related to both **reliability** and **validity** in a study because:

- **Standardised procedures** and **scripted behaviour** reduce the amount of personal decision-making researchers have to make
- Tried-and-tested **instruments**, like established **questionnaires** and **observational schedules** as well as **scientific instruments**, like **brain imaging techniques**, ensure results do not depend on personal interpretation
- Strongly **experimental methods** with **controls** and **quantitative data** produce results that eliminate researcher bias

The opposite of objectivity is SUBJECTIVITY. In subjective research, the results are based on the researcher's personal interpretation and may reflect his or her biases.

There's a debate within Psychology about the importance of objectivity. Researchers who value the SCIENTIFIC STATUS of psychological research are strongly in favour of objectivity.

However, some argue that research into human experience must always be subjective to some extent and we should accept subjectivity rather than trying to fight it at the cost of robbing our research of **ecological validity**. Moreover, research that ignores subjectivity is more likely to become UNETHICAL because the human factor is being left out.

Research into EYEWITNESS TESTIMONY aims for great objectivity: **Elizabeth Loftus** carries out lab experiments with **standardised procedures** and **controls** (such as filmed car crashes to watch, hidden leading questions and quantitative data). These studies aren't very realistic but Loftus' own interpretations and biases are excluded.

Research involving biological measures (such as **genetic testing** or **brain imaging**) is quite objective because these results are scientific facts.

However, there is still some interpretation that goes into understanding a PET SCAN or identifying what genes are responsible for what, so subjectivity cannot be entirely ruled out even in the most scientific research.

The GOOD LIVES MODEL has been criticised by **Andrews *et al.* (2011)** for its subjectivity. Normal cognitive-behaviour treatments have very focused and carefully defined goals for clients to aim for but GLM instead uses vague life goals like 'Peace of Mind'. How can we know whether clients are making progress towards subjective goals like this? **Don Andrews** calls GLM:

> *a return to unstructured professional judgement* – **Don Andrews**

CREDIBILITY

Credibility refers to the PERSUASIVENESS of a study or instrument: ***does it offer a convincing explanation or measurement?***

Credibility is related to **reliability**, **validity** and **objectivity** in a study because:

- **Standardised procedures** and **scripted behaviour** add to credibility by making research more REPLICABLE and less SUBJECTIVE
- Tried-and-tested **instruments**, like established **questionnaires** and **observational schedules** as well as **scientific instruments**, like **brain imaging techniques**, are credible because they have been used successfully by previous researchers
- Strongly **experimental methods** with **controls** and **quantitative data** produce results that are credible because CONFOUNDING VARIABLES have been ruled out

Many psychologists interpret credibility as being the same as having SCIENTIFIC STATUS: a credible piece of research will be persuasive because it has stuck to scientific procedures. The PEER REVIEW PROCESS is important for **scientific credibility**. This is when a scientific research paper is sent out to reviewers before it is published. The reviewers check the findings and look for bias that might undermine the conclusions. If they find the research to be unbiased and free from flaws, they approve it for publication.

Peer review is time-consuming and a lot of research is rejected: the famous journal ***Science*** only accepts 8% of the research studies submitted for its peer review process.

There are criticisms of the peer review process. The SOKAL AFFAIR (1996) is a famous hoax where scientist **Alan Sokal** submitted a bogus (and nonsensical) article with a lot of fancy terminology to a scientific journal. After it was published, he revealed the hoax.

Peer review seems to be at risk of TYPE I ERRORS: reviewers are likely to approve research from famous scientists or tackling popular or trendy topics, even if the research lacks credibility in other ways.

There are OPEN ACCESS JOURNALS that do *not* peer review studies: either the researcher pays a fee or the editor publishes studies he or she thinks have value. This is a good way for unusual, obscure or controversial research to get published.

John Bohannon (*Who's Afraid of Peer Review?* 2013) submitted fake scientific papers with serious flaws to 304 open-access journals and found 60% were published: these studies would never have passed a peer review process. This questions the credibility of research that *doesn't* go through peer review.

All of the research studies in this book are peer-reviewed.

Some research passes the peer review process but still fails to persuade other scientists (for example, if the results are surprising or contradict established theories). These scientists will test the research by REPLICATING it to see if the same findings occur. Research that is successfully replicated has a lot of credibility. However, published research that conforms to people's prejudices or expectations isn't like to be challenged and replicated.

Gesh *et al.* (2002, p35) was a peer-reviewed study published in the ***British Journal of Psychiatry***. Gesh's findings – that a diet supplement reduces violence among young offenders compared to a placebo group – is surprising, even a bit weird. **Zaalberg et al. (2005, p35)** replicated the research in a Dutch prison (with slight changes) and came up with similar results, suggesting Gesh's findings *are* credible.

One way of identifying credible studies is a META-ANALYSIS which reviews lots of existing research to establish the overall findings (**concurrent validity**). For example, **Mier & Ladny (2017**, p20**)** reviewed 42 studies over 25 years and found a **negative correlation** between SELF-ESTEEM and youth offending which makes other research linking low self-esteem with crime more credible.

Similarly, **Köhnken *et al.* (1999, p45)** also reviewed 42 studies and found the COGNITIVE INTERVIEW to be superior to standard interviewing, which makes CI more credible.

ETHICS IN CRIMINOLOGICAL PSYCHOLOGY

You were introduced to ethical guidelines for researchers as part of Unit 1. The **BPS Code of Ethics (2018)** emphasises **respect**, **competence**, **responsibility** and **integrity**. These principles are put into practice in the following ways:

Guideline is...	Meaning	Advantage	Disadvantage
Consent	Participants must make an INFORMED CHOICE to take part	Informed participants understand what will happen to them	It's not possible to inform children or some people with autism if they lack language or self-awareness
Deception	Participants must not be misled by researchers	Honest researchers can be trusted and establish a good reputation	It may be necessary to deceive participants to avoid DEMAND CHARACTERISTICS
Withdrawal	Participants must be able to leave a study (or have their data deleted) without justifying why	Withdrawing participants have AUTONOMY and are protecting themselves	Children and some people with autism may lack the language or social skills to withdraw
Protection	Participants must not be harmed and must leave in the same state they entered	This shows RESPECT for unharmed participants and establishes a good reputation	Some research will always be stressful for participants but stress does not have to lead to permanent damage
Confidentiality	The identities of participants should be kept secret	Protects participants from association with SOCIALLY SENSITIVE issues	Some participants generate intense media interest (e.g. Genie) or would shed more light if identified (e.g. Little Albert)
Debriefing	All the details of the study should be explained at the end	This can make up for necessary deception (up to a point)	It's not possible to debrief young children or severely autistic participants
Competence	Researchers must not make or imply claims they are not qualified to do (e.g. diagnosis)	Prevents alarming parents by suggesting their children have a disability	Parents may assume researchers are competent (e.g. as doctors or psychiatrists) even though they don't claim to be

BPS Guidelines make it clear that children under age 16 cannot give informed consent and are especially at risk in psychological studies. However, parents or guardians can give PRESUMPTIVE CONSENT (consenting *on behalf of* the child).

APPLYING HCPC TO CRIMINOLOGICAL PSYCHOLOGY

The HEALTH & CARE PROFESSIONS COUNCIL (HCPC) is an organisation regulating practitioner-psychologists – people who use psychological skills as part of a job. Forensic Psychologists are practitioner-psychologists and if they wish to work for the UK Prison Service or alongside the UK Police they must be registered with the HCPC.

A psychologist needs to re-register with the HCPC every 2 years. It is a criminal offence to claim to be HCPC registered if you are not.

The HCPC imposes 15 'standards' on its members. Three of these include:

- Being able to practice with the **legal and ethical boundaries** of the profession
- Being able to practice in a **non-discriminatory** manner
- Understanding the importance of **confidentiality**

Legal & Ethical Boundaries

Because they often work alongside offenders, forensic psychologists may face pressure to break the law themselves. This can include providing drugs for prisoners, withholding information about crimes that a prisoner confesses to during treatment and passing information on to the prisoner's associates on the outside which assists in carrying out or covering up crimes. Often this pressure comes as a request for a 'favour'. Psychopaths are particularly manipulative.

HCPC forensic psychologists must maintain **legal boundaries** and refuse to break the law themselves: this means refusing to help prisoners acquire drugs, declining to pass on messages and making sure information about crimes is always passed on to the police. Since forensic psychologists often need to establish a *RAPPORT* (relationship of trust) with a prisoner, this can cause problems, but the psychologist has to make their position clear right at the beginning of any treatment or research.

There are also **ethical boundaries**, such as not entering into romantic or sexual relationships with prisoners.

> *If you think that's unlikely, look up the Daily Mail's 2008 story:* ***Married prison psychologist fell pregnant after affair with mentally-ill inmate.*** *Stephanie Reeves lost her job after sex with the schizophrenic convict she was counselling in a secure unit.*

Non-discrimination

Forensic psychologists conduct CASE FORMULATION, which advises courts and parole boards whether a criminal should be kept in prison or released. Obviously, advice like this should not discriminate against offenders based on any aspect of their life:

> *treating others differently because of your views about their lifestyle, culture or their social or economic status, as well as ... age, disability, gender reassignment, race, marriage and civil partnership, pregnancy and maternity, religion or belief, sex and sexual orientation* – **HCPC Guidelines**

Discrimination can take subtle forms. For example, using the word *"gang"* rather than *"group"* in records often indicates that the offenders are Black/Minority Ethnicity (BME, source: **Lammy Report, 2017**). **Islamophobia** in the media can influence psychologists to discriminate against Muslim convicts and **transsexual** prisoners continue to experience discrimination.

An example of a study taking steps to avoid discrimination is **Whitehead *et al.* (2007, p31, 33)** who provided a Maori counsellor who would relate to Mr C's Maori culture.

Confidentiality

Forensic psychologists can learn a lot about offenders, either from studying court records or interviewing them directly. The HCPC states that this information must not be shared with others. This means

- It cannot be included in **published research**
- It cannot be shared with **friends, family or colleagues** or put on **social media**
- It must be kept in a **secure location** (e.g. locked filing cabinet, password-protected computer)

However, the HPCP allows for some exceptions:

- If the psychologist has **permission** (e.g. **Mr C** gave consent for **Whitehead *et al.*** to publish his details but not his real name)
- It is in the **public interest**, including public safety (this includes passing on information to the police if a crime is revealed)
- It is in the **client's best interest** (this includes passing on details to health workers about mental disorders, drug abuse, self harming, etc.)

Because of these exceptions, psychologists should never promise their clients complete confidentiality: they have a legal and moral obligation to pass on some information.

REVISING METHODOLOGY & ETHICS

DEFINITIONS
CONFIDENTIALITY
CREDIBILITY
HCPC
META-ANALYSIS
OBJECTIVITY
PRESUMPTIVE CONSENT
RELIABILITY
SUBJECTIVITY
VALIDITY

RESEARCH SUMMARIES
BOHANNON (2013)
THE SOKAL AFFAIR (1996)

COMPREHENSION QUESTIONS
1. How does inter-rater reliability improve research?
2. Why are case studies often unreliable?
3. What is the difference between construct validity and concurrent validity?
4. How can research be made more valid?
5. What is the advantage of meta-analyses?
6. Why is ecological validity a problem for research into eyewitness testimony?
7. What is the problem with subjective research?
8. How can research e made more credible?
9. What are the problems with research using children?
10. Why is it important to be a member of the HCPC?
11. How could a forensic psychologist be 'struck off' by the HCPC?
12. Why is it difficult to maintain confidentiality in forensic psychology

RESEARCH
Find out more about methodological issues in Psychology at **theguardian.com**:
- *Study delivers bleak verdict on validity of Psychology experiment results* (Sample, 2015)
- *Psychology experiments are failing the replication test – for good reason* (Ioannidis, 2015)
- *Are all psychological therapies equally effective?* (Freeman & Freeman, 2014)
- *The changing face of Psychology* (Chambers, 2014)
- *Psychology's 'registration revolution'* (Chambers, 2014)
- *Open science is now the only way forward for Psychology* (Chambers, 2018)

EXAM-STYLE QUESTIONS

The Health & Care Professions Council (HCPC) regulates practitioner-psychologists in the UK and forensic psychologists must meet its standards in their work.

(a) Outline one standard promoted by the HCPC. [2 marks AO1]

(b) Explain how a forensic psychologist might keep this standard. [4 marks AO2]

(c) Evaluate issues of credibility in criminological psychology. [8 marks AO1+AO3]

DATA ANALYSIS

Data analysis was introduced in Unit 1 and developed in **Unit 2A (Clinical Psychology)**. The main points will be revised here but only **Grounded Theory (GT)** will be considered from the perspective of Criminological Psychology.

Quantitative data is...	Meaning	Advantage	Disadvantage
Measures of central tendency	The different types of 'averages' (mean, median and mode)		
Mean	Add up all the values and divide by the size of the set	Useful with interval/ratio level data	May be a value that isn't actually in the set; may be distorted by outliers
Median	The central value when the set is arranged in rank order	Useful with ordinal level data	Doesn't reflect outliers; no actual median if the set is even-numbered
Mode	Most frequent value in the set	Useful with nominal level data	May be several modes or none
Measures of dispersion	Scores showing how the set is spread out (range, standard deviation)		
Range	Highest score minus lowest score	Shows whether there are outliers	Doesn't show how many outliers there are
Standard deviation	Deduct the mean from each score, square the result, divide the sum by the size of the set minus 1, take the square root	Shows how far away from the mean a score has to be to count as unusual	Only useful if there is a mean (interval/ratio level data)

The Specification also singles out FREQUENCY TABLES. These are charts that show how often behaviours occur as a column of varying heights. Unlike a simple bar chart, ***the columns are touching***. The **mode** will appear on a frequency table as the highest column(s).

This frequency table shows the frequency of letters appearing in English words. Can you spot the mode (the letter that appears most frequently in words)?

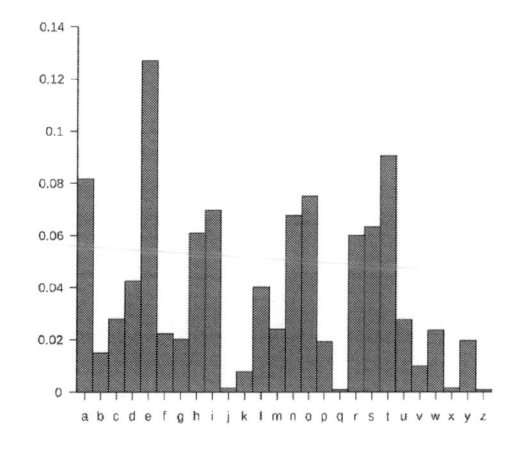

81

Statistics are...	Meaning	Advantage	Disadvantage
Inferential tests	Statistical tests that show how a probable or typical a set of data AS A WHOLE is compared to the wider population		
Mann-Whitney U	Compared to the critical value: if lower, the results are significant	Independent groups experiments + ordinal level data	Cannot be used with nominal data; unreliable with small ($\leq$5) samples
Wilcoxon	Compared to the critical value: if lower, results are significant	Repeated measures experiments + ordinal level data	Cannot be used with nominal data; unreliable with small ($\leq$5) samples
Spearman's Rho	Compared to the critical value: if higher, the results are significant	Used with correlations + ordinal level data	Cannot be used with experiments; doesn't show cause-and-effect
Chi Squared	Compared to the critical value: if higher, results are significant	Independent groups experiments + nominal level data	Cannot be used with ordinal data
Statistical significance	Whether the observed value shows a meaningful difference (experiments) or correlation or whether they are down to chance		
Interval/ratio level	Data where each participant has their own score	Mean can be calculated; can be converted to ordinal level data	Not all behaviours or traits can be expressed as scores; may be REDUCTIONIST
Ordinal level	Data where participants are arranged in rank order, highest to lowest	Median can be calculated; used for Mann-Whitney, Wilcoxon & Spearman	Not all behaviours or traits can be ranked from best to worst; tends to be REDUCTIONIST
Nominal level	Data where behaviours are put into categories (usually as tallies)	Mode can be calculated; used for Chi-Squared	Doesn't show individual scores or performances
Critical value	Score from a statistical table against which the observed value (result of a the test) is compared	Indicates the point where chance variations become signs of a pattern or difference	Critical value varies depending on the LEVEL OF SIGNIFICANCE (probability is usually $p \leq 0.05$)

ISSUES OF STATISTICAL SIGNIFICANCE are covered in **Unit 1**. The typical level is **$p \leq 0.05$** which means *the probability of a chance outcome is 1 in 20 (5%) or less*. Changing the level of significance alters the critical value. The smaller the value of *p*, the more probable it is that there is a statistical pattern at work.

GROUNDED THEORY (GLASER & STRAUSS, 1967)

Grounded Theory (GT) is a technique for drawing themes out of qualitative data in a systematic way. It tries to reduce the SUBJECTIVITY (opinion rather than fact) in qualitative data and make the conclusions more OBJECTIVE (factual) while still keeping the depth and detail of qualitative data.

GT was developed by **Glaser & Strauss** while they were researching the experiences of terminally ill patients. Interviewing dying patients is SOCIALLY SENSITIVE so the researchers created this technique to let the patients 'speak for themselves' and avoid imposing their own biases on the data.

GT works by identifying key points in the interview and identifying these with codes. Later, the codes are grouped into similar concepts and categories (referred to as **themes** elsewhere in this course). The researchers create memos (e.g. on file cards) to explore how these categories relate to each other and identify the CORE CATEGORY, which is the basis for a new theory.

This theory is **emergent**: it 'emerges' out of the data rather than being something you start off with. GT can be evaluated in terms of **fitness** (do they 'fit' the data well?), **relevance** (do they tie in with what the respondent feels and wants?), **workability** (can you put them to use?) and **modifiability** (can later research find improve on them?).

- **Lopez & Emmer (2000)** used GT to study the emotions and cognitions of 24 young offenders through interviews
- **Clark (2011)** used GT to study how Maltese gangsters explain their criminal lifestyle
- **De Brie & De Poot (2016)** used GT to analyse Dutch police files on *jihadist* (Islamist) terror networks

> *You don't need to know much about these studies but it would be good to be able to cite at least one in a discussion of GT*

EVALUATING GROUNDED THEORY IN CRIMINOLOGICAL PSYCHOLOGY AO3

Glaser and Strauss later disagreed over the role of TRANSCRIPTS in GT. Transcripts are when you write/type up the interview afterwards (creating something that reads like a script of a play). **Barney Glaser** argues that it is time-consuming to create a transcript and you lose the *rapport* (emotional connection) when working from a transcript. **Anselm Strauss** argues that it's easier to come up with codes and write memos when working from a transcript and trying to do these things during the actual interview gets in the way of *rapport* anyway.

This disagreement shows that GT is not a STANDARDISED PROCEDURE (compared to content analysis, for example). This lowers its reliability, because it is hard to replicate, and questions the SCIENTIFIC STATUS of its conclusions.

However, GT is growing in popularity among researchers. **Kathy Charmaz (2006)** has done a lot to bring different approaches to GT together into a usable system. Carmaz adds ORIGINALITY to the ways of evaluating emerging theories:

> *Are your categories fresh? Do they offer new insights?* – **Kathy Charmaz**

GT is useful for interviewing offenders because it allows the researcher to carry out a natural-sounding **unstructured interview** with someone who might be unwilling to open up. It can create **concepts and categories** even if the offender has a limited vocabulary or expresses themselves through gestures, facial expressions or drawing. In terms of the **HCPC**, GT is very useful for reducing **discrimination** in psychological research.

The idea of an **emergent theory** goes against the way scientific research is usually doe (starting with a hypothesis which is tested). GT instead starts with a blank piece of paper and gathers data without trying to fit it into a theory until later. GT aims:

> *to discover the theory implicit in the data* – **Barney Glaser**

This makes GT less useful for testing an established theory (the way **Zaalberg** tested **Gesh**'s theory that diet might be responsible for violent offences). However, it can be useful for generating brand new theories because it sets aside biases and preconceptions.

For example, **Eysenck** and **Freud** both went into their research with a theory in mind. **Hans Eysenck** (p21) expected to find prisoners score high for P (PSYCHOTOCISM) and **Sigmund Freud** expected to find unconscious conflicts in his patients. Both have been accused of 'cherry picking' their data to get it to back up their theories. If they had used GT instead (if it had existed back then), they might have come up with completely different theories instead!

However, GT might be just a new name for something researchers have always done. **Hans Eysenck** developed his idea of **personality traits** (E, N and later P) through interviewing battle-fatigued soldiers in a military hospital; **Robert Hare** developed his concept of the PSYCHOPATH from interviewing Canadian prisoners who seemed to be particularly unfeeling and resistant to correction. These men didn't call their approach 'grounded theory' but it seemed to lead to the same results.

REVISING DATA ANALYSIS & GROUNDED THEORY

DEFINITIONS
INTERVAL/RATIO LEVEL DATA
MEAN
MEDIAN
MODE
NOMINAL LEVEL DATA
ORDINAL LEVEL DATA
P≤0.05
RANGE
TRANSCRIPT

WHEN WOULD YOU USE:
CHI-SQUARED
MANN-WHITNEY U TEST
SPEARMAN'S RHO
STANDARD DEVIATION
WILCOXON TEST

RESEARCH
Carry out your own Grounded Theory analysis of a short passage:

- The Howard League for Penal Reform website has diary extracts written by real prisoners

howardleague.org/what-you-can-do/transform-prisons/prison-diaries/

COMPREHENSION QUESTIONS
1. What are the measures of central tendency?
2. What are the problems with using the mean?
3. What are the measures of dispersion?
4. What is meant by statistical significance?
5. Where do you find a critical value?
6. Which is the stricter test, P≤0.05, P≤0.01 or P≤0.001 ?
7. How do you produce ordinal level data?
8. What sort of data is produced by tally marks in boxes?
9. Who developed Grounded Theory?
10. What is the point of memos in GT?
11. What disagreements are there in using GT?
12. Outline a study that uses GT in Criminological Psychology.

EXAM-STYLE QUESTIONS

Heidi tests eyewitnesses on the number of details they correctly recall from a video of a simulated robbery. She scores the number of correct details each eyewitness recalls.

(a) Calculate the mode in these scores. [1 mark AO2]

(b) Calculate the standard deviation for these scores. [4 marks, AO2]

(c) Use standard deviation to identify the outliers in these scores. [2 marks AO2]

Participant	Number of correctly recalled details
1	7
2	2
3	6
4	7
5	10
6	2
7	0
8	7
9	5
10	5

CRIMINOLOGICAL PSYCHOLOGY: STUDIES

What's this topic about?

For your Exam you will need to know about a **classic study** in Criminological Psychology:

- ☐ **Loftus & Palmer (1974):** *Reconstruction of automobile destruction*

Because every candidate studies the same classic study, exam questions on it might be quite specific (e.g. asking you about the specific questions Loftus asked).

You will also need to know 1 **contemporary study** and there are 3 to choose from:

- ☐ **Bradbury & Williams (2013):** *The Effects of Race on Juror Decision Making*
- ☐ **Valentine & Mesout (2009)** *Eyewitness identification in the London Dungeon*
- ☐ **Howells *et al.* (2005)** *Brief anger management programs with offenders*

Because the Examiner doesn't know which contemporary study each candidate has learned, exam questions on the contemporary studies have to be much broader (e.g. just asking for the findings, the procedure or the aims).

> *However, the **classic** or **contemporary study** could feature in a 16-mark essay question, with up to 10 marks for evaluation (AO3). Therefore, in the next few pages I'll devote space to evaluating these studies rather than describing their procedures or findings in depth.*

WHICH CONTEMPORARY STUDY TO CHOOSE?

- ☐ **Bradbury & Williams (2013)** is a simple study with simple findings. It makes a good extra study for JURY DECISION-MAKING. However, it requires some understanding of the rather complex procedures for jury-selection in the USA. Some candidates might prefer a more complex study with a simpler background.
- ☐ **Valentine & Mesout (2009)** looks at factors affecting EYEWITNESS TESTIMONY, notably stress and gender. It's a useful methods study because it contrasts with lab experiments into EWT and **Yuille & Cutshall**'s famous field experiment (p70). It also introduces two questionnaires to measure stress. It's a memorable study, but probably the most complicated one in terms of procedure and findings.
- ☐ **Howells *et al.* (2005)** is longitudinal study looking at the effectiveness of OFFENDER TREATMENT PROGRAMMES, such as anger management. It has a simple procedure, but involves several questionnaires and has some confusing results. It's probably the dullest and least memorable of the three studies.

CLASSIC STUDY: LOFTUS & PALMER (1974)

Reconstruction of automobile destruction is a **lab experiment** (p 60) which investigates the effect of POST-EVENT INFORMATION on EYEWITNESS TESTIMONY (p40).

> *Elizabeth Loftus is probably the biggest name in eyewitness testimony research: there are countless websites and textbooks discussing her studies and theories.*

AIM

Loftus wanted to investigate the effects of **leading questions** on eyewitnesses: whether the wording of a question would make them recall a car crash at a higher or lower speed. She also tested whether other aspects of memory would be affected by the wording.

PROCEDURE

45 American students were shown 7 road safety films of car crashes (each lasting 5-30 seconds) then given a questionnaire with 9 **distractor questions** and 1 **critical question** about the final crash: "*How fast were the cars going when they hit each other?*"

The IV was the wording of the critical question: 9 participants were asked "*hit each other,*" 9 "*smashed into each other,* 9 "*collided with each other,*" 9 "*bumped into each other,*" and 9 "*contacted each other.*" The DV was the speed estimate. No one knew the other participants were being asked differently-worded questions.

Loftus then recruited 150 students, showing them a 1-minute car crash film and giving them the same questionnaire. This time 50 participants were asked "*How fast were the cars going when they hit each other?*" and 50 read "*smashed into each other*" and the other 50 didn't get a question about the speed at all (CONTROLS with unaltered memories). Loftus gathered these participants again a week later for more questions, one of which was "*Did you see any broken glass?*" (the answer should have been 'No').

RESULTS

Word used	Mean Estimate of Speed	False recall of broken glass
Smashed	40.8 mph	32%
Collided	39.3 mph	-
Bumped	38.1 mph	-
Hit	34.0 mph	14%
Contacted	31.8 mph	-
No question	-	12%

> *You don't need to memorise the entire table, but revise a couple of stand-out figures from it, like 40.8mph/32% for 'Smashed' vs 34mph/12% for 'Hit'.*

The more intense the verb used (from the gentle *"contacted"* through the moderate *"hit"* and *"bumped"* up to the violent *"smashed"*), the faster participants recalled the cars to be travelling. This shows the effect of leading questions.

The second experiment shows that the intense leading question (*"smashed"*) causes participants to remember broken glass when there wasn't any. There was no significant difference between *"hit"* (14%) and the control group (12%), so a certain amount of false recall is normal – but the difference for *"smashed"* (32%) can only be due to the wording.

CONCLUSIONS

This supports the MISINFORMATION EFFECT (p41): when eyewitnesses receive POST-EVENT INFORMATION, this causes them to revise their memory without realising it. They estimate the cars to be going faster and this activates SCHEMAS (fast car crashes are associated with greater destruction) and this causes them to remember things that weren't there (like broken glass).

> *It's important to remember that the 50 people in the "smashed" condition saw the film and got asked the speed question a WEEK PREVIOUSLY but this* **still** *affected their memory.*

GENERALISABILITY

This study suffers from the common problem of a sample of university students who might have superior powers of recall but might be relatively inexperienced at driving or judging car speeds (older people would be more likely to have been in a car crash at some point).

RELIABILITY

This is a **standardised procedure** that is easy to REPLICATE (the fixed questions, the same films of car crashes). In a way, Loftus *did* replicate it when she ran the second experiment using the same questions as the first but adding the 'broken glass' question a week later.

In fact the study *was* replicated in Canada by **Yuille & Cutshall (1986, p70)** but as a **field experiment**, using an actual street shooting rather than a filmed car crash. Instead of broken glass, 13 witnesses to the shooting were recruited 4 months later and asked if they saw *"the broken headlight"* (there wasn't one) and 10/13 correctly said 'No.'

> *So* **Yuille & Cutshall** *replicated* **Loftus & Palmer** *but got opposite results.*

APPLICATION

The study suggests juries and judges should be cautious about trusting eyewitnesses in court. The **Devlin Report (1976)** instructs judges to warn all juries that even confident eyewitnesses could be mistaken and recommends that no defendant should be convicted on the basis of a single unsupported eyewitness testimony.

The study also suggests that police officers and lawyers who interview eyewitnesses should be trained not to ask leading questions in case they 'contaminate' the witness with post-event information.

VALIDITY

The study has **construct validity** (it is supported by SCHEMA THEORY) but lacks **ecological validity**. Watching filmed car crashes is not like being an eyewitness to a real crash because there is no drama, fear or concern for people's safety. Real eyewitnesses have to be careful to get details right (it might affect whether someone gets an insurance payout or goes to prison) but there was nothing at stake for Loftus' participants.

Yuille & Cutshall got different results, which lowers **concurrent validity** for the study. Yuille & Cutshall were studying real witnesses to a shocking shooting. This has high ecological validity as the witnesses had recently been interviewed by the police.

ETHICS

There are no major ethical issues with this study, since no one witnessed a real accident and the road safety films were intended to be shown to the general public.

FURTHER REFLECTIONS

Loftus' research is highly OBJECTIVE, since it gathers quantitative data that requires no personal interpretation: either the participants recalled correctly or they did not. Her research is widely viewed as CREDIBLE and her criticisms of EWT are taken very seriously. Elizabeth Loftus is called to be an 'expert witness' in court and advise juries about EWT.

What then should be made of the contradictory results from **Yuille & Cutshall**'s replication? Yuille & Cutshall (p70) isn't a perfect replication. The witnesses had been interviewed (several times) by the police and had arrived at a very consistent version of the shooting. 8 other eyewitnesses did not take part in the study and these might have been the ones with more uncertain memories of the incident.

Brown & Kulik (1977) propose that there a special types of memories called FLASHBULB MEMORIES. These are created by very intense experiences and they are particularly long-lasting and accurate. Yuille & Cutshall were testing a flashbulb memory (a shooting) but Loftus was not (a film of a car crash). So Loftus' conclusions might be true for ordinary memories, but not for traumatic flashbulb memories.

However, **Hirst *et al.* (2015)** surveyed witnesses to the 911 terror attack on New York, 10 days after the event, then 1, 3 and 10 years later. '911' would definitely qualify as a flashbulb memory but the study found over the years the witnesses dropped to only 60% accuracy compared to their first response. This suggests flashbulb memories *feel* vivid but aren't actually any more reliable than normal memories.

CONTEMPORARY STUDY 1: BRADBURY & WILLIAMS (2013)

Effects of race on juror decision-making is an American study by **Mark Bradbury & Marian Williams**. It is a **natural experiment** (p60) comparing JURY DECISION MAKING (p53) in trials of Black defendants where the jury is mostly White, Black or Hispanic.

AIM

Identify how the decisions made by juries about Black defendants vary based on the racial makeup of the jury. The researchers also have a wider aim of exploring whether inequalities in US society can e reduced by making juries more diverse.

PROCEDURE

Data was used from 382 real trials of Black defendants in 2000-2001 in the **Bronx** (a poor area of New York with an equal mix of Black and Hispanic), **Los Angeles** (a city in California with an equal mix of White and Hispanic), **Maricopa** (a small city in Arizona with a majority White population) and **Washington DC** (the US capital with an equal mix of White and Black). The trials were all 'non-capital felonies' (i.e. no murders or killings).

CONTROLS were used to make the trials comparable. The trials were matched on (1) the amount of evidence (e.g. number of witnesses), (2) the strength of the prosecution's case, (3) the length of the trial, (4) how long the jury deliberated, (5) whether the jury was given special instructions by the judge.

> *Getting this sort of data on real trials is rare.* **Bradbury & Williams** *used data made available to a previous (2002) study into the problem of hung juries in America*

The IV is the race of the jury (majority White, Black or Hispanic) and the DV is whether the defendant was convicted or the jury was deadlocked (hung trial). No trials were used where the defendant was found innocent.

RESULTS

A conviction (guilty) was coded 1, a deadlock (hung trial) or no conviction was coded 0 and LOGISTICAL REGRESSION was used (a statistical test similar to correlation but using **nominal level data**).

Jury is	Likelihood of conviction of Black defendant compared to majority-Black jury
Majority-White	Higher ($p \leq 0.01$)
Majority-Hispanic	Slightly higher ($p \leq 0.1$)

As a level of probability, **p≤0.01** for majority-White juries is well above chance, but **p≤0.1** for majority-Hispanic juries is only slightly above chance. For *any* sort of jury, Black defendants are slightly more likely to be convicted of drug crimes compared to violent or property crimes (**p≤0.1**, so only marginally significant).

CONCLUSIONS

The research suggests that the ethnicity of the defendant does make a difference to jury decision-making when the majority of jurors have a different ethnicity. This applies regardless of the quality of evidence, the strength of the case against the defendant, the time taken and the behaviour of judges and lawyers. Furthermore, Black defendants are more likely to be convicted in cases of drug-related crimes.

GENERALISABILITY

Investigating Black defendants makes the study generalisable, because the researchers note that they made up 60% of the defendants in all the trials available in the 4 regions (with Whites making up 10% and Hispanics 24%).

However, for the same reason this study is not representative of trials involving White, Hispanic or other defendants. For example, Baltimore is a city with a thriving Greek community, Jersey City has the highest concentration of Asian Indians in the USA while Framingham, Massachusetts is said to be 57% Brazilian.

382 trials is a lot for a Psychology study, but every year there are 100 million cases brought to State Courts in America, so the sample is a tiny proportion of the target population. The four State Courts were chosen for the early 2002 research precisely because they were unusual (a high number of hung trials). This means they are likely to be unrepresentative of felony trials generally.

The results will not be representative of other countries. **Thomas (2010)** did not find bias in British juries, perhaps because Britain does not share the US history of slavery.

RELIABILITY

The procedure involved using a data file from an earlier 2002 study into hung juries, so in a way this study is itself a REPLICATION of an earlier study, investigating the same data in more depth. The data is historical and available for checking, so it has **inter-rater reliability**.

However, the data was over a decade old when the research was conducted. Crime figures have changed since then: overall, the US crime rate has dropped every year since 2001. If the data were gathered again today, it might show different trends – but gathering this sort of data is difficult unless State Courts cooperate, so this study lacks **test-retest reliability**.

APPLICATION

Bradbury & Williams make the obvious suggestion that lawyers representing Black defendants should try to get their client judged by a majority-Black jury.

Bradbury & Williams also recommend that American society should become more equal through public participation in things like juries. If more Black Americans did jury duty (and fewer of them were removed from juries during the VOIR DIRE process), Black defendants would suffer less discrimination in court.

VALIDITY

Similar to the UK study by **Thomas (2010**, pp54, 55**)**, this study has **ecological validity** because it uses real jurors. However, it is even more realistic than that because it takes data from real trials, not simulated trials. The findings tie in with SOCIAL IDENTITY THEORY, which claims that jurors will see defendants of their own race as an in-group (and judge them more leniently) and defendants of a different race as an out-group (and judge them more harshly).

ETHICS

This study uses historical data from decade-old trials so there are no ethical issues.

FURTHER REFLECTIONS

This study requires some knowledge of the US courts, which randomly call citizens up for jury duty. The jurors join a 'jury pool' which is then reduced to the 12 who actually sit in the jury. A VOIR DIRE (pronounced "*vwah-deer*") hearing is when the prosecution and defence lawyers challenge potential jurors by dismissing them from the jury pool. Commonly, jurors are challenged if they might prejudice the trial because of their views or loyalties. However, these PEREMPTORY CHALLENGES are often used to create a jury that is biased one way or the other.

Trial lawyers know (from previous studies and professional experience) that Black defendants are more likely to be convicted by non-Black juries, so the prosecution team makes a point of challenging and dismissing Black jurors from the jury pool.

> *In the UK, the prosecution can ask biased jurors to 'stand down' and be replaced by someone else before the trial. However, this power is rarely used. Peremptory challenges were removed from the British legal system in 1988 because they were seen as unfair.*

Bradbury & Williams show evidence that supports juries being racially biased in their decision-making. This has the additional application of calling for reform of the US legal system to produce more diverse juries, perhaps by abolishing peremptory challenges before trials begin.

CONTEMPORARY STUDY 2: VALENTINE & MESOUT (2009)

Eyewitness identification under stress in the London Dungeon is the title of this study by **Tim Valentine & Jan Mesout**. It is a **natural experiment**, testing the impact of anxiety and gender on recall in a field setting (the 'London Dungeon' which is a tourist attraction famous for its scary theme).

AIM

Determine if AROUSAL (physical excitement due to stress) affects memory recall and whether this happens more in men or women. The researchers also tested whether the STATE ANXIETY INDEX (SAI, a psychometric text measuring temporary feelings of stress) **correlated** with biological measures of stress (heart rate).

PROCEDURE

56 visitors to the London Dungeon were offered a reduced rate for agreeing to fill in questionnaires after their visit and wear a wireless heart monitor. There were 29 females and 27 males, aged 18-54 (mean age 31). The visitors spent 7 minutes exploring the 'Horror Labyrinth' (a creepy maze with sinister sounds and sudden frights). An actor in a dark robe with fake scars (the 'Scary Person') would appear suddenly to frighten visitors.

45 minutes later, the visitors left the Dungeon and completed the SAI to record their feelings of stress and the TRAIT ANXIETY INDEX (TAI) to rate their normal levels of anxiety. They were asked to recall a description of the 'Scary Person' and then pick the actor playing the 'Scary Person' out of a photo line-up of 9 images. The photo of the 'Scary Person' was placed in a random position among the 8 'foils' and the participants were warned that the person they saw might not be in the line-up. After making a selection, the participants rated their certainty on a scale of 0%-100% confidence.

RESULTS

There was a **positive correlation** ($p \leq 0.001$, so very significant) between heart rate and scores on the SAI, which suggests the SAI is a **valid** measure of stress and arousal. On average, State Anxiety was higher than the score on the TAI, which shows that people were feeling unusually aroused by their experience in the London Dungeon.

There was a **negative correlation** ($p \leq 0.01$, so significant) between participants' score on the SAI and their number of correct descriptions of the 'Scary Person' (e.g. height, age), so the more stressed they felt the less well they recalled.

On average, females scored higher for stress than males (**$p \leq 0.01$**) and were less likely to identify the 'Scary Person' in the line-up (**$p \leq 0.005$, so very significant**).

There was a positive correlation (**p≤0.001**, very significant) between confidence and correctly identifying the 'Scary Person'.

The MEDIAN score on the SAI was 51.5 so anyone scoring lower than this was 'Low Arousal' and anyone higher 'High Arousal'. Low Arousal showed much greater success in identifying the 'Scary Person' (**p≤0.001**) and High Arousal resulted in more failures to make any identification at all.

Number of eyewitnesses (/56)	Anxiety (mean SAI score 49.0)		Sex of eyewitness	
	Low (<51.5)	High (>51.5)	Male (mean 45.3)	Female (mean 52.8)
Correctly identify Scary Person	21	5	19	7
Identify other 'foil'	6	15	5	16
No identification made	1	8	5	4

You don't need to know all the numbers. Make a note of the 21 correct IDs in the Low Arousal condition and the 19 correct IDs from men, who are on average likely to be in the Low Arousal group with a mean SAI score of 45.3.

CONCLUSIONS

Anxiety and stress affects the accuracy of eyewitness recall: participants who were in the lower half of the SAI scores were 75% likely to correctly ID the 'Scary Person' in the line-up but those in the upper half were only 17% likely to get it right. There was a link between confidence and correct ID, suggesting that eyewitnesses know when they are recalling correctly.

GENERALISABILITY

The sample was a mix of males and females and a mix of ages and the tourist attraction was a popular one where a representative sample might be found. The fact that the participants showed raised levels of State Anxiety after going through the Dungeon suggests they were responding normally to the stress and tension of the experience..

RELIABILITY

The study had carefully scripted questions for the participants (such as how they were asked to describe the 'Scary Person') and used two well-established psychometric tests: the TAI (which measures how anxious your personality is) and the SAI (which measures the particular level of stress you are feeling at the moment).

However, the behaviour of the 'Scary Person' was not so carefully scripted. The participants were pointed out to the actor, who would to block the visitor's way.

Different actors played the 'Scary Person' on different occasions and some might have been more imposing than others or improvised intimidating gestures or facial expressions. Some actors might have been more distinctive and easier to recognise.

APPLICATION

Valentine & Mesout are concerned to prevent innocent people being wrongly convicted by mistaken eyewitnesses. Police could be informed that stressed eyewitnesses are less reliable at picking out an offender from a line-up. Perhaps allowing time to pass between the crime and identifying the offender would allow stress levels to drop (although it would also allow POST-EVENT INFORMATION to contaminate the recall).

Juries might be advised that female eyewitnesses are less reliable when stressed. However, this is a SOCIALLY SENSITIVE issue. There is currently a concern that female witnesses are not believed and men who attack women are not convicted, so this sort of research might only make it harder for female plaintiffs to get justice in court.

VALIDITY

Although it is not a field experiment (the IV is **naturally-occurring** and not manipulated by the researchers), this study has a real-world setting that causes participants to be in a state of real (although mild) stress. This is more realistic than most lab experiments into EYEWITNESS TESTIONY. Valentine & Mesout compare their study to **Yuille & Cutshall (1986**, p70**)** and point out that their participants were tested for recall soon after meeting the 'Scary Person', whereas Yuille & Cutshall waited 4 months after the crime.

ETHICS

The participants agreed to take part in a survey but were not told about the 'Scary Person' so they did not give INFORMED CONSENT. However, since they came to the London Dungeon to seek out a scary experience (and would have complained if they didn't get one!), there is PRESUMPTIVE CONSENT that the participants *would have consented* if they had been asked. The 'Scary Person' seemed to be a normal part of the attraction, so the participants were not subjected to stress beyond what they expected.

FURTHER REFLECTIONS

Valentine & Mesout suggest more ideas for testing real stress on eyewitnesses: at a fairground ride (e.g. a 'big dipper' or rollercoaster) and doing an extreme sport (e.g. bungee jumping). This is a move away from traditional **lab experiments** like **Loftus & Palmer (1974**, p87**)** and towards greater realism but remaining ethically acceptable because participants have chosen the stressful activity themselves. However, such research cannot demonstrate cause-and-effect the way a lab experiment can.

CONTEMPORARY STUDY 3: HOWELLS *ET AL.* (2005)

Brief anger management programs with offenders is a study led by Australian psychologist **Kevin Howells**. It is **a natural experiment** comparing prisoners receiving ANGER MANAGEMENT THERAPY with prisoners who had not yet started treatment.

AIM

Determine whether **anger management therapy** is more effective than no treatment in changing behaviour. Also, to discover whether **pre-treatment characteristics** in offenders help predict whether anger management therapy will be effective.

PROCEDURE

The study used 418 prisoners in Australia, with sentences ranging from 1 month to 26 years. The mean age was 28.8 and the majority (65%) were Australians or New Zealanders, but 19% identified as Aboriginal or Islanders. Most (73%) had never completed an anger management course before.

A well as comparing 285 prisoners receiving anger management with a non-treatment CONTROL GROUP, the researchers used a longitudinal design to follow up on 78 prisoners two months later and 21 prisoners six months later.

The anger management course ran for 10 two-hour sessions. The focus was on identifying 'trigger' situations for anger, relaxation and assertiveness training (to express anger constructively, without violence). Lots of questionnaires were used to monitor progress. The main ones were:

- SPIELBERGER STATE-TRAIT ANGER EXPRESSION INVENTORY (STAXI) to measure feelings of anger, anger as a personality trait and angry behaviour
- WATT ANGER KNOWLEDGE SCALE (WAKS) to measure how successful they are at understanding and dealing with anger
- SERIN TREATMENT READINESS SCALE (STRS) which is a combined questionnaire and interview to measure how ready they are for treatment

> *It's nice to know the full names but you can get by with just the abbreviations: STAXI, WAKS and STRS.*

RESULTS

There was a slight improvement detectable 2 months after treatment (+1.5 in controlling anger compared to +0.5 for controls) and the treatment group improved their understanding of anger (+1.8 on WAKS compared to +0.95) which is significant at $p \leq 0.05$.

These results are mostly *not* significant so the researchers looked for a **correlation** between how psychologically readiness (STRS) and aggression scores (STAXI).

Scores on STAXI	Correlation with STRS:	
	Control Group (no treatment)	Anger Management Group
State Anger (feelings)	-0.1	+0.16
Trait Anger (personality)	+0.05	-0.26
Expressed anger (behaviour)	+0.26	-0.25

The most significant difference is the negative correlation of -0.26 in Trait Anger (personality) for the anger management group compared to +0.05 for the controls. This is significant at **p≤0.001**.

CONCLUSIONS

The overall impact of the anger management course was small and possibly no better than chance. However, it did offer offenders a better understanding of their anger. Offenders who were motivated to change showed the biggest improvement but those who were not psychologically ready for the course showed little or no improvement.

GENERALISABILITY

The sample is reasonably large and contains a mixture of ethnicities and types of prisoner (including those with short and long sentences), so it should be representative of Australian prisoners generally and anomalies (such as PSYCHOPATHS) won't skew the data.

However, it only looks at Australian males. Possibly anger management courses have more success with women or men in other countries. Remember that **Kilham & Man (1974)** replicated **Milgram's obedience study** in Australia but found only 28% of participants went to 450 V (compared to 65% in America). It's possible Australians are particularly resistance to authority and this might include anger management too.

RELIABILITY

The questionnaires used are all well-established psychometric tests. The anger management course itself was designed by **Raymond Novaco (1997)** who is a pioneer in the field of anger management.

Charles Spielberger (1991) is another pioneer of anger management and created the STAXI test, which has 57 Likert-style questions on angry feelings and dispositions and takes 10-15 minutes to complete. It is widely used in prisons.

Kroner & Reddon (1992) tested the STAXI for **test-retest reliability** with prisoners and found a **strong correlation** of 0.64 for Trait Anger (personality) between the first test and a second test a week later.

APPLICATION

The study suggests anger management courses are a waste of time unless focused on particular prisoners who are ready for change. The STRS test can be used to measure psychological readiness and prisoners who score high on this could be put forward for anger management courses, since they are most likely to get something out of it.

VALIDITY

This sort of research has a problem with SOCIAL DESIRABILITY BIAS: the prisoners would want to present themselves as improving because of the course if they believed (rightly or wrongly) that it would help their chance of getting parole or other privileges.

Howell *et al.* counteract this by using 6 different questionnaires to measure changes in the prisoners: even if the prisoners 'cheat' at one or two questionnaires, they won't be consistent across all of them. This gives the results **concurrent validity**.

ETHICS

The prisoners all volunteered to take part in the study. The control group were not deprived of the chance of treatment: they received their anger management course after the experimental group. This means everyone was treated fairly. The results show that prisoners did receive some (small) benefit from doing the course.

FURTHER THOUGHTS

This study shows you that not all psychological research comes up with exciting findings and not all experiments find a significant difference between conditions. It also illustrates how researchers can interrogate statistical data closely to find interesting patterns (like the correlation between readiness and improvement in Trait Anger) even when there are no obvious differences.

In the UK, the anger management course used in prisons is CALM (stands for Controlling Anger & Learning to Manage It).

CALM is controversial. Critics say that these courses only help offenders conceal and focus their ager, making them more effective criminals. In 2006, the UK Government scaled back anger management courses after Damien Hanson murdered a man while robbing his house. Hanson was a recently-released prisoner who had attended 24 sessions of an anger management, which helped convince the parole board he had had a "*change of heart*" and was no longer dangerous.

> *After the Hanson case, the UK Government concluded that anger management should be focused only on prisoners who are likely to benefit from it – which is the same conclusion Howells et al. reached the previous year (without anybody being murdered).*

REVISING CLASSIC & CONTEMPORARY STUDIES

DEFINITIONS: LOFTUS & PALMER
CRITICAL QUESTION
RECONSTRUCTIVE MEMORY

DEFINITIONS: BRADBURY & WILLIAMS
LOGISTICAL REGRESSION
VOIR DIRE

DEFINITIONS: VALENTINE & MESOUT.
AROUSAL
SAI
TAI

DEFINITIONS: HOWELLS *ET AL.*
ANGER MANAGEMENT
STAXI
STRS
WAKS

TICK YOUR CONTEMPORARY STUDY
- ☐ BRADBURY & WILLIAMS (2013) Effects of race on juror decision-making
- ☐ VALENTINE & MESOUT (2009) Eyewitnesses in the London Dungeon
- ☐ HOWELLS *ET AL* (2005) Brief anger management programmes

COMPREHENSION QUESTIONS
LOFTUS & PALMER
1. What effect did the verb have on estimates of speed?
2. What evidence is there that schemas were responsible for the false memories?
3. What was the difference between the two experiments?

BRADBURY & WILLIAMS
4. What was the sample?
5. How do majority-White juries respond to Black defendants?

VALENTINE & MESOUT
6. How was stress-arousal measured?
7. How did men and women differ in their recall?
8. What explanations are there for this?

HOWELL *ET AL.*
9. What was the sample?
10. Explain whether anger management has any benefits for prisoners.

RESEARCH
Find out about cases of false memory in court, such as the case of **George Franklin** that involved Elizabeth Loftus.
Alternatively, research the **'Super Recognisers'** who work for London's Metropolitan Police.

EXAM-STYLE QUESTIONS

As part of Child Psychology, you learned about the classic study by Loftus & Palmer (1974).

(a) Describe the findings (results and/or conclusions) of this study relating to the recall of broken glass at the car crash. [4 marks AO1]

(b) Explain one strength and one weakness of the study's samples. [4 marks AO3]

(c) Evaluate the contemporary study you learned about for Criminological Psychology. [8 marks AO1+AO3 or 16 marks AO1+AO3]

CRIMINOLOGICAL PSYCHOLOGY: KEY QUESTIONS

What's this topic about?

For the Exam, you need to know about

> *one issue of relevance to today's society, explaining the issue and applying concepts, theories and/or research (as appropriate) drawn from criminological psychology* – **Edexcel Specification, p31**

Two examples are offered:

- ☐ Is eye-witness testimony too unreliable to trust?
- ☐ Should jury bias lead to the abolishment of juries?

> *Notice that this is a KEY QUESTION and these really are QUESTIONS. If the Exam asks you to write your Key Question, you won't get marks unless you write it as a question, not just "eyewitnesses" or "jury bias"*

For your Key Question, you must be able to

- show some **real-world knowledge** of these topics (not studies or theories but actual news events, Government policies or statistical trends in society)
- show how **psychological studies or theories** explain these real-world facts

> *This is important. If you just treat the Key Question as an essay on "the psychology of eyewitness testimony" or "the psychology of jury bias" you will lose a lot of marks.*

The next two pages offer 4 'facts' for each of the suggested Key Questions. Students could research these facts a bit further. There are also pointers to the psychological theories and studies in this book that link to these 'facts'.

KEY QUESTION 1: Is eye-witness testimony too unreliable to trust?

FACT 1: Eyewitnesses suffer cryptomnesia

The case of Donald M. Thompson, who was identified as a rapist by a woman her saw his face on TV during a sex attack, shows that eyewitnesses can substitute information from one memory into another, without being aware they have done so.

- **Psychology link:** What research suggests memory is reconstructive and can be changed after-the-event?

FACT 2: Eyewitnesses experience false memories

The case of George Franklin, who was accused of rape and murder by his own daughter based on a memory recovered during a hypnosis session, shows that there can be 'false memories' of events that never happened.

- **Psychology link:** What research supports the idea of false memories created from schemas?

FACT 3: Innocent people have been convicted due to unreliable eyewitnesses

The case of Ed Honacker, who was convicted of rape after being identified from a photo line-up by an eyewitness but released after 10 years in prison thanks to DNA evidence, shows that unreliable eyewitnesses lead to miscarriages of justice.

- **Psychology link:** What research supports the idea that eyewitnesses might false accuse people due to stress, weapon focus or faulty police questioning?

FACT 4: Some eyewitnesses are more reliable than others

Not all eyewitnesses are equally unreliable. The Metropolitan Police has a team of 'super recognisers' who are officers with exceptional ability to recognise faces. PC Gary Collins can pick out suspects from grainy CCTV that he last saw years ago. During the London Riots in 2011, these officers were able to identify hundreds of suspects from CCTV.

- **Psychology link:** What research suggests some types of memory might be very vivid or long-lasting? Are there gender differences in memory? What techniques help improve the memory of eyewitnesses?

KEY QUESTION 2: Should jury bias lead to the abolishment of juries?

FACT 1: Juries are biased against certain ethnicities

In US courts, it has been illegal to 'strike' (remove) jurors because of race since 1986, but lawyers find other ways round this and Black Americans are still underrepresented on juries. Meanwhile, all-White juries are 16% more likely to convict a Black defendant than a White defendant.

- **Psychology link:** What research suggests juries are biased against certain ethnicities? Which theories explain this bias??

FACT 2: Juries are biased in favour of attractive people

Lawyers know to advise their clients to dress attractively when appearing as witnesses, plaintiffs and defendants. The serial killer Ted Bundy, who murdered more than 30 young women in the USA in the 1970s, was physically attractive and wanted to represent himself in court to benefit from his charm.

- **Psychology link:** What research suggests juries are influenced by attractiveness?

FACT 3: Juries are influenced by pre-trial publicity

In 2002, the lawyer David Corker called for a ban on pre-trial publicity, saying that journalists had a *"licence to kill"* by influencing juries with their reporting. In the USA, the First Amendment guarantees freedom of speech, so journalists cannot be silenced and legal teams respond by giving press statements and hiring publicity agents.

- **Psychology link:** What research suggests PTP influences juries?

FACT 4: Juries can overcome their biases if alerted to them

If media coverage creates substantial prejudice against a defendant, a conviction can be regarded as 'unsafe' and 'quashed' by an Appeal Court. However, judges often advise juries to set aside biases and concentrate only on the evidence presented in court.

- **Psychology link:** What research suggests that instructions from a judge encourage juries to be unbiased?

CRIMINOLOGICAL PSYCHOLOGY: PRACTICAL INVESTIGATION

What's this topic about?

To prepare for the Exam, you need to

> *conduct a questionnaire, interview or an experiment* – **Edexcel Specification, p32**

Two examples are offered:

- ☐ An experiment into the use of cognitive interview concerning recall of a specific event.

- ☐ View a crime/courtroom drama and conduct an interview/questionnaire on participants about the reasons why the defendants may have committed the crime they are accused of.

> *Notice that you are advised to interview an ADULT. The Examiner expects you to follow BPS Guidelines and not to carry out research on children under 16.*

For your Key Question, you must be able to

- Gather quantitative data and carry out an inferential statistical test
- Describe the hypotheses being tested, sample, procedure & instruments used, results and conclusions
- Discuss the strengths, weaknesses and possible improvements

> *This is important. The Exam is more likely to ask you to EVALUATE your Practical than it is to ask you to describe what you did or what you found.*

The next two pages offer guidelines for carrying out the suggested Practicals. You only need to do one and you should keep it as simple as possible. Make sure you understand **why** you are doing what you are doing by answering the questions too.

PRACTICAL 1: Experiment into effectiveness of the Cognitive Interview technique

HYPOTHESIS

Participants will score significantly higher on a recall test using CONTEXT REINSTATEMENT compared to a recall test in a different context.

- Is this 1-tailed or 2-tailed? Design a null hypothesis based on this.

SAMPLE

Either gather an opportunity sample of students at your Centre or a volunteer sample of friends or family. Make sure everyone gives informed consent and is 16+.

- Examine the critical value tables (at the start of each Exam Paper): how many participants do you need to carry out a successful inferential test?

INSTRUMENTS

If you search on YouTube or Google Video for simulated+crime you will find a suitable video (there's a good Australian simulation called **Film 1** that is 1:28 in duration)

Create a 10-question recall test about the video.

Show the film to a group. Test half the group in the same location and seating arrangement (Context Reinstatement); test the other half in a different room with different seating.

INFERENTIAL TEST

Use Mann-Whitney U Test to assess the difference between the two sets of scores.

- Why is Mann Whitney U the appropriate test to use in this case?

DISCUSSION

Evaluate your sample: How would a different sample size, target population or sampling technique have improved things?

Evaluate the video used: Does it pose ethical problems? Does it resemble a real crime? Could an observation of an acted crime have produced a better test?

Evaluate the questions asked: Are they realistic for an actual crime interview? Are the participants in a similar frame of mind to real eyewitnesses? How could this be improved?

PRACTICAL 2: Survey on viewers' explanations for criminality

HYPOTHESIS

There will be a difference between the number of male and female participants who attribute biological explanations compared to social explanations for a defendant being tried for a crime in a court room scene.

- Is this 1-tailed or 2-tailed? Design a null hypothesis based on this.

> *Instead of male/female, you could compare older/younger or science/arts*

SAMPLE

Gather an opportunity sample of students or a volunteer sample of friends or family. Make sure everyone gives informed consent and is 16+.

- Examine the critical value tables (at the start of each Exam Paper): how many participants do you need to carry out a successful inferential test?

INSTRUMENTS

A 10 minute US court room scene can be found on YouTube and Google Video: **Court Room Scene from Law and Order The Family Hour**

After watching the film clip, viewers must choose between a biological explanation (e.g. genes) or a social explanation (e.g. labelling by media). You could offer the participants two explanations to choose between (avoiding psychological terminology) and possibly add distractor questions about other aspects of the trial.

> *You could use clips from other films, but avoid violent or sexual content (especially trials for rape or child abuse).*

INFERENTIAL TEST

Use Chi-Squared Test to measure a difference between males and females.

- Why is Chi-Squared Test the appropriate test to use in this case?

DISCUSSION

Evaluate your sample: How would a different sample size, target population or sampling technique have improved things?

Evaluate the questions asked: Do any pose ethical problems? Are any of them vague or misleading? Would it be better to use a real trial rather than a scene from a TV drama?

CRIMINOLOGICAL PSYCHOLOGY: ISSUES & DEBATES

What's this topic about?

These 11 'Issues & Debates' can feature as part of a question in **Unit 2B (Criminological Psychology)** as well as a question related to Applications in **Unit 3 (Issues & Debates)**.

COMPARING EXPLANATIONS WITH DIFFERENT THEMES

Biological explanations involve genes, which lead to brain structures that influence decision-making and emotion. These genes are passed on through natural selection because they have SURVIVAL VALUE but there are also random mutations. For example, the XYY chromosome and MAOA 'warrior gene' are mutations. However, biological pressures can only be towards broad classes of behaviour (like risk-taking or impulsiveness) not specific crimes.

Social explanations involve labels and stereotypes, which are INTERNALISED to become part of a person's SELF-IMAGE. These forces come from society, through the attitudes of parents, teachers and the police as well as messages in the media and pressure from peer groups. However, this does not explain where labels come from in the first place and why some people can resist or avoid labels but others cannot

Interactionism brings these themes together, arguing that biological factors give us a PREDISPOSITION towards criminality, but social situations determine whether or not we act on those urges in a criminal way. This link to the idea of RECIPROCAL DETERMINISM, otherwise known as the 'vicious circle' when social labels encourage us to be bad and our bad behaviour makes society label us negatively, or the 'virtuous circle' when good behaviour creates positive labels.

CULTURE

A culture is a group of people united by common norms, beliefs and practices. For example, British culture unites people are norms like politeness and drinking tea, beliefs in democracy and individualism and practices like football, following soap operas and eating fish & chips. There are also SUB-CULTURES, which are groups within the wider culture who share distinctive beliefs and behaviours in common.

Criminal sub-cultures might **reinforce** (reward) criminal behaviour, offer antisocial SCHEMAS (such as crime being fun) and present criminal **role models** to imitate (p25).

ETHNOCENTRISM is the belief that your own group is normal or natural, e.g. that other cultures or sub-cultures are criminal but yours is not. This could explain the tendency of all-White juries to convict more Black defendants – and the tendency of all-Black juries to be lenient towards Black defendants.

The **Sherif 'Robbers Cave' study** shows how working towards **superordinate goals** reduces ethnocentric bias. This might explain the finding in **Thomas (2010**, pp54, 55**)** that all-White juries in multicultural Nottingham were more likely to convict a White defendant than a Black one (because the jurors work alongside non-White people in their daily lives).

ETHICS

Ethics are rules that oblige us to ensure the wellbeing of other people (and also animals). Ethical guidelines were developed by the **British Psychological Society (BPS)** in 1974 but these are supplemented by the **Health & Care Processions Council (HCPC, p78)** standards. These ethical codes insist that participants give informed consent to research involving them, are not deceived or put at risk and are debriefed afterwards.

Mock juries and experiments in EYEWITNESS TESTIMONY usually involve a lack of **informed consent**, because participants have to be kept in ignorance of the aspect of the defendant (e.g. attractiveness) or testimony (e.g. critical question) being investigated. However, this can be addressed during **debriefing** and these studies don't usually involve any **risk** to the participants

Research into OFFENDER TREATMENT usually requires a **control group** that does not receive the treatment being investigated (or else a **placebo group** that receives an ineffective version of the treatment). This means some prisoners are being deprived of a treatment which is being offered to others, which is unfair.

NATURE-NURTURE

'Nature' is a term for aspects of human identity that we are born with (INNATE) whereas 'nurture' is a term for aspects of identity that we learn from our environment. Human identity seems to be a mixture of nature e.g. our genes) and nurture (e.g. our upbringing) but psychologists debate which is more influential.

Biological explanations of crime tend to focus on the nature-aspect. They show that mutated genes (like XYY chromosomes or the MAOA mutation) can be present from birth and cause antisocial behaviour, including crime.

Brain deficits (e.g. in the **amygdala**) are less clear-cut because these can come about based on experience rather than being present from birth; this is the concept of **brain plasticity** where the brain changes its structure based on the things humans spend a lot of time doing.

Social explanations show us how society causes criminality by stereotyping and labelling people from an early age. However, these theories do not explain why some people identify with negative labels (the SELF FULFILLING PROPHECY) while others fight against them (the SELF-DENYING PROPHECY). This difference might be rooted in PERSONALITY, which could be **natural** rather than a product of upbringing.

PRACTICAL ISSUES IN DESIGNING RESEARCH

Criminological Psychology has some distinctive problems: we do not know in advance when crimes are going to occur so we cannot study criminals before they commit crimes or eyewitnesses immediately after the event. The law prevents researchers studying juries directly (that would be **Contempt of Court**) and many police forces are unwilling to cooperate fully with psychological research while they are investigating cases. The only criminals researchers have access to are those in prison, who may not be representative of offenders still at large.

Psychologists get round these problems with LAB EXPERIMENTS into EWT, **mock juries** to investigate jury decision-making and CASE STUDIES into particular criminals, crimes or police forces. However, all these techniques are "second best" to researching the real thing and suffer from problems with **generalisability** and **ecological validity**.

Occasionally, researchers get an unusual opportunity to bypass these restrictions. **Thomas (2010)** uses real jurors and courtroom scenes with the cooperation of the Government. **Yuille & Cutshall (1986)** use real eyewitnesses to a street shooting.

PSYCHOLOGY DEVELOPS OVER TIME

Early Criminological Psychology is dominated by ideas that have been discredited, such as **Lombroso**'s theory of criminal body types. Even relatively modern ideas such as XYY SYNDROME have been replaced, first by the arrival of brain imaging techniques like PET SCANS and then by the boom in genetic research in the 1990s and the discovery of genes like the MAOA-variant. Because of these breakthroughs, the **biological explanation** of criminality has become the dominant model.

Instead of looking for a single explanation that covers all crime, researchers are increasingly proposing **interactive** models that show how factors like biology, social environment and personal combine together

The main debate in Criminology is over the treatment of offenders. Cognitive-behaviour techniques like anger management are very widespread and popular with prison services, but there are concerns that these types of counselling do not challenge the worst behaviour. In fact, they sometimes teach prisoners how to be more successful criminals. New techniques like the GOOD LIVES MODEL have emerged to tackle the sort of offenders who do not respond to ordinary counselling.

REDUCTIONISM

Reductionism is reducing an explanation of human behaviour to a simple level to understand it better. This can be done through reducing human traits to number scores (quantitative data) or putting human behaviour into one of a small number of categories or types. Reductionism is an essential component of SCIENTIFIC explanations.

Criminological Psychology is reductionist when it reduces offenders to bundles of genes or brain structures, defines eyewitness testimony through number scores (e.g. Loftus' estimated speeds) or defines defendants entirely by their attractiveness, ethnicity or gender (often while ignoring social class). Psychometric tests like **Hare's Psychopathy Checklist** (**PCL**, p22 can be seen as reductionist as is **Eysenck's**'s classification of personality in terms of E, N and P traits (p21).

However, psychologists are alert to the danger of this and now try to include as many variables as possible in their research. The big **longitudinal** studies like **CDDS** (p16) gather data on the physical, emotional and mental traits, the home background, the parents' relationships, etc. as well as criminal records.

SCIENTIFIC STATUS

Science is a method for investigating the world in an OBJECTIVE (detached, factual) way. Scientific research tests HYPOTHESES to develop THEORIES which account for things in a systematic, rules-based way. It is a very successful way of discovering truth and solving problems.

Psychology is termed a 'social science' but there are problems with studying scientifically. Humans are RESPONSIVE and react to what you do to them; they are MORALLY SIGNIFICANT which restricts what you are allowed to do with them; and they are AUTONOMOUS which means they can choose how to act rather than being governed by simple laws of cause-and-effect.

From the work of **Lombroso** onwards, Criminology has tried to develop more and more scientific ways of studying the nature of offending while still respecting the responsive, morally significant and autonomous nature of offenders and eyewitnesses. For example, **Raine *et al.* (1997)** takes pains to explain that the distinctive brain deficits found in murderers do *not* show that they were 'born that way' or that they lack freewill.

SOCIAL CONTROL

Criminological Psychology aims to reduce the destructive impact of crime: preventing it in the first place, improving ways of identifying suspects and convicting the guilty and developing techniques to help prisoners change their destructive ways. Psychology tries to use this power for good – but it can be used for evil as well.

Since states get to define what is and isn't a crime, in some countries things like expressing your political views, religious ideals or sexual preferences can be criminalised. This means the same psychological techniques for catching and convicting murderers and making sure they don't reoffend can also be used to persecute political protesters, religious minorities and sexual orientations like homosexuals and transsexuals.

SOCIAL SENSITIVITY

This is when research has implications that go beyond participating in the study itself, either long-term harm for the participants or harmful influence on society itself.

Biological explanations risk portraying 'biology as destiny' and creating prejudice against the biological relatives of offenders (who share their genotype) or a mistaken prejudice against whole racial groups who are viewed (mistakenly) as having a biological predisposition to crime.

Psychology has a role in uncovering and preventing injustices, such as **Elizabeth Loftus** exposing false memories and **Gary Wells** exposing innocent people convicted due to unreliable eyewitnesses (p40). However, Psychology can add to false perceptions if it supports the idea that certain ethnic groups are more likely to be criminals, certain juries are biased in their decisions or certain witnesses are unreliable. A good example is the debate over the difficulties faced by women accusing men of rape. Often this boils down to one person's word against another, but research that suggests memories of sex attacks might be **confabulated** or that women make poor eyewitnesses under stress only makes it harder to secure convictions of real rapists.

USEFULNESS IN SOCIETY

For a long time, Psychology had little impact on the Criminal Justice System (CJS): courts followed ancient rituals and police officers stuck to their own traditional practices which meant newfangled ideas (like the COGNITIVE INTERVIEW) met with a lot of resistance.

Police forces adopted psychological techniques, first with facial composites (like **IdentiKit** ad **PhotoFit**, more recently **E-FIT**) to help eyewitnesses pick out suspects. More recently, cognitive-behavioural treatments for offenders have become common in prisons, like the CALM programme for anger management (p98). The COGNITIVE INTERVIEW is gaining acceptance among police forces, largely with a push from the UK Government's PEACE programme for ethical interviewing.

It remains to be seem how useful genetic and neurological (brain-based) explanations of offending will be. **Adrian Raine** argues that PET scans could help courts and parole boards work out which offenders need to be imprisoned and which can be safely released into the outside world.

REVISING KEY QUESTIONS, PRACTICALS & ISSUES

DEFINITIONS
CULTURE
ETHICS
INFERENTIAL TEST
HYPOTHESIS
NATURE-NURTURE
NULL HYPOTHESIS
OPERATIONALISE
PRACTICAL DESIGN ISSUES
PSYCHOLOGY OVER TIME
REDUCTIONISM
SCIENTIFIC STATUS
SOCIAL CONTROL
SOCIAL SENSITIVITY
SOCIAL USEFULNESS
TEST OF DIFFERENCE

TICK YOUR KEY QUESTION
☐ IS EYEWITNESS TESTIMONY TOO UNRELIABLE TO TRUST?
☐ SHOULD JURY BIAS LEAD TO THE ABOLISHMENT OF JURIES?

TICK YOUR PRACTICAL
☐ EXPERIMENT IN EFFECTIVENESS OF COGNITIVE INTERVIEW
☐ SURVEY ON VIEWERS' EXPLANATIONS OF CRIMINAL BEHAVIOUR

EXAM-STYLE QUESTIONS

(a) Discuss the key question you have researched in Criminological Psychology. [8 marks AO1+AO2]

(b) (i) Explain the method (aims and/or procedures) you used in your Criminological Psychology practical [3 marks AO2]

(ii) Explain two weaknesses in your Criminological Psychology Practical and how you could reduce them if you replicated the research. [4 marks AO2+AO3]

(c) Evaluate research in Criminological Psychology in terms of social sensitivity. [8 marks AO1+AO3]

(d) Assess the extent to which offending is due to nurture rather than nature. [8 marks AO1+AO3]

(e) Assess the usefulness to society of research into eyewitness testimony. [8 marks AO1+AO3]

(f) Assess the extent to which biological explanations of criminality are more persuasive than other explanations. [16 marks AO1+AO3]

ABOUT THE AUTHOR

Jonathan Rowe is a teacher of Religious Studies, Psychology and Sociology at Spalding Grammar School and he creates and maintains **www.psychologywizard.net** and the **www.philosophydungeon.weebly.com** site for Edexcel A-Level Religious Studies. He has worked as an examiner for various Exam Boards but is not affiliated with Edexcel. This series of books grew out of the resources he created for his students. Jonathan also writes novels and creates resources for his hobby of fantasy wargaming. He likes warm beer and smooth jazz.

Printed in Great Britain
by Amazon